# A Tale of Two Basketball Towns and Their Coach Jim Musburger

1

# State Champs '48

**Bemidji High School Lumberjacks 1948 State Basketball Champs:
Jack Horne, Jim Musburger, Ross Fortier (assistant coach's son)
Chet Aakus, Chuck Grover, Jim Sexton, Dick Calhoun, Dick Leach,
Bud Gordon, Wes Sabourin, Lyle Goodspeed** (1948 Lumberjack)

*There is a quote that says: "A good coach can change a game. A great coach can change a life." For me this couldn't be truer about my High School Basketball Coach.* – Tom Porter '79, Karlstad

Cover photo 1968 Karlstad Bluebook

# A Tale of Two Basketball Towns and Their Coach Jim Musburger:

# Strandquist and Karlstad, Minnesota 1956 – 1979

Memories from Coach Jim Musburger,
Athletes and Fellow Coaches

by Jill Musburger Johnson '70

**Dedicated to Coach Jim Musburger, athletes, fellow coaches and fans**

**Jim Musburger, Bemidji Lumberjacks Varsity Football 1947-48**
(1948 Lumberjack)

# ACKNOWLEDGEMENTS

Many wonderful athletes, coaches, cheerleaders and friends helped with the stories in the project. Thank you to all the athletes who shared their stories: Harlan Bengtson, Neal Benson, Chester Boen, Paul Bostrom, Don Carlson, Dan Clark, Troy Dagen, John Erickson, Mark Erickson, Kragh Folland, David Grandstrand, Kent Hanson, David Henry, Randy Hultgren, Sheila Nordine Jeanotte, Chris Johnson, Jim Johnson, Ken Johnson, Betty Kasprowicz, Richard "Pete" Kasprowicz, John Keller, Randy Krantz, Kevin Kuznia, Mike Kuznia, Doug Larson, Conrad Lubarski, Wayne Lutz, Jeff Musburger, Jim Musburger Jr., Mark Newman, Diedre Nordin, Jan Nordin, Jon Nordine, Greg Oistad, Keith Olson, Loel Olson, Tim Olson, Ernie Pietruszewski, Jerry Pietruszewski, Richie Pietruszewski, Tim Porter, Tom Porter, Allen Rasmussen, Dan Sele, Lee Sele, Brian Sjodin, Lowell Sjodin, Neil Skogerboe, Eldon Sparby, David Spilde, Rodney Stromlund, Jerry Szczepanski, Ken Urbaniak and Wesley Vagle. A special thank you to Tim Olson '67, who initiated the project, and to Allen Rasmussen '61 and Jerry Szczepanski '61 who tirelessly sent Strandquist history. Thanks to the coaches who coached with and against Jim Musburger-they all have great stories: George Bunn, Karl Carlson, Phil Johnson, Bill Margerum, Larry Peterson, John Schmidt, Gary Schuler, Ron Ueland, Jim Schindele, Jerry Snyder, Todd Pack, Duane Heck, Dick Moen and Eldon Sparby. Louis Deere and Warren Keller, great coaches and friends of Jim Musburger, are deceased and their unforgettable legacy is cherished forever by sports fans.

A huge shout out to Cindy Adams at the Kittson County Museum for photos, to Gretchen Baker and Rollin Bergman at the *North Star News* (*Karlstad Advocate*) and *Middle River Record* for access to their archives and permission to use photos and articles, the *Grand Forks Herald* for the story and photo of the Musburger coaches and the photo of Warren Keller, and the *Bemidji Pioneer* for the 1948 Lumberjack team photo. Mavis Gonshorowski and Ryan Bergeron from the *Greenbush Tribune* provided information from the *Middle River Record*. Scott Marthaler (LeMar Photography), Bill Champa (Champa Studio), and Scott Cooper (Cooper Studio), generously allowed inclusion of Strandquist, Karlstad and Bemidji yearbook photos–thank you. Thanks to Ken and Keith Urbaniak for Louis

Deere's photo and to Sharon and John Keller for Warren Keller's photo. Ryan Baron, Tri-County Superintendent, gave permission to use information from the Strandquist and Karlstad yearbooks.

My gratitude to Greg and Jodie Olson, Kathy Britten, Gail Rasmussen, Darlene Gryskiewicz, Val Pietruszewski, Polly Spilde, Julie Spilde, Virginia Johnson, Joyce Wikstrom and Colette Kuznia, who dug through dusty yearbook annuals and newspaper archives for photos and information.

A heartfelt thank-you to Dane Nordine, publisher of the *North Star News (Karlstad Advocate),* who wrote with great feeling and eloquence for "the boys." His writing speaks to the joy and pride in a community infused with the camaraderie of sports. Although Dane died in 1997, his writing lives on in the history of our towns.

My brother, Jim, and sister, Julie, stood with me through the project and remembered events through their own personal lens. My mom, although gone several years, remains a constant presence in our lives and in dad's memories. Thanks to Deane, my fantastic technology wizard, who makes all things possible.

Foremost, thanks to Coach Jim Musburger, our inspiration and force for excellence in life. You made us better people.

# A TALE OF TWO BASKETBALL TOWNS
# AND THEIR COACH JIM MUSBURGER

## TABLE OF CONTENTS

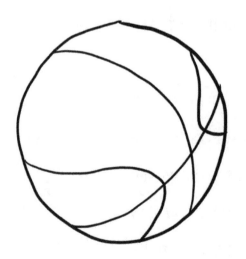

# INTRODUCTION

*For twelve years I had a front row ticket to one of the greatest shows on the planet. The Musburger/District 32 show gave me status, pride, joy, and thousands of memories of great teammates, great opponents, great fans, and great coaches. It gave me health and strength, it gave me goals, it gave me confidence.*
– Loel Olson '77

This is the story of two basketball teams and their coach, Jim Musburger, who coached and taught in Strandquist and Karlstad, two small towns in northwestern Minnesota from 1956 to 1979. They were single-minded in their pursuit of excellence and good sportsmanship, in a way unique to small town basketball and other sports as well. Before computers, cell phones and video games, basketball, often the only winter sport in small towns, provided countless thrills and excitement for players, fans and coaches. Stories of small-town sports are endlessly retold around the country, but the stories are fading as small schools dissolve. Strandquist, like many schools in northwestern Minnesota, closed in 1991, and the Warriors consolidated with Karlstad, another small town seven miles north. As enrollment dropped in Karlstad, the school consolidated their sports programs with Newfolden in 1990, and the Rabbits are now the Northern Freeze. At one time, District 32 in northwest Minnesota had 16 teams, seven in the east: Baudette, Roseau, Warroad, Badger, Greenbush, Middle River and Newfolden, and nine in the west: Humboldt, Lancaster, Lake Bronson, Hallock, Karlstad, Kennedy, Strandquist, Stephen and Argyle. Now the total number is down to seven teams. For decades, a steady caravan of fan buses and cars traveled through blizzards, sub-zero temps and floods to follow their treasured team and pack high school gyms in remote Minnesota. Along the way, athletes, fans and coaches cemented friendships, strengthened the town's commitment to their youth and earned the respect of their communities.

The Warriors and the Rabbits are now history but their spirit and pride live on in all the athletes, coaches and fans, who poured their hearts and souls into every game. The stories, told by Coach Jim Musburger, his athletes and fellow coaches, recall the impact of small town sports and a coach on their lives and communities. An unusual attribute of this book is that the coach and many of his players and peers are alive to tell stories from their perspective. Dane Nordine, our hometown newspaper publisher, wrote: *"Sports are a wonderful thing, and there are some wonderful people in them."*

When Tim Olson '67 suggested that I collect stories about Jim Musburger, his high school basketball and assistant football coach, I wasn't sure I was up to the task. Coach Musburger is my father and although I had heard multiple stories over the years, this project would be possible only if his athletes and others connected to his career would share their memories from 1956 to 1980, a lifetime ago. These special young men and colleagues held the key to his successful coaching career and shared experiences known only to them. Typical of Jim Musburger's entire coaching career, his athletes and peers came through for him and ended up writing the book in their own words.

Jim Musburger, born in 1930, grew up on Beltrami Avenue in downtown Bemidji, Minnesota, during the depression. The fourth of six children, he, along with all his siblings, began working at a young age. He owned his own shoeshine shop downtown, caddied at the golf course and shagged golf balls. Known as "Muzzy," the red head played football and basketball for the Bemidji Lumberjacks. In 1948, the Bemidji basketball team, coached by Mike Lagather and Bun Fortier, made school history when they defeated Hopkins 38 – 29 for the state high school championship in the era of one-class basketball. Jim is one of the few survivors of that glorious team.

Following high school graduation, Jim enlisted in the Air Force at age 17 and boarded the train for basic training at Lackland Air Force Base in San Antonio, Texas. He recalls shaking his father's hand at the train station - no demonstrative affection in a tough German Catholic family. Three years later, he returned to marry his high school sweetheart, Adeline Melhus, and they moved to Arlington, Virginia, to finish out Jim's final year in the Air Force. Jim wanted to marry Adeline earlier but his parents would not sign for the underage pair as she was Lutheran and refused to baptize their future children in the Catholic faith. When Jim asked his commanding officer for permission to marry, he replied, "Why don't you wait until you are fifty? Then

10

you won't have to suffer so long."  But he did approve the marriage and the young couple took the train to Washington, D.C. to finish Jim's military service at Fort Belvoir.  When they stepped off the train, Jim had 35 cents in his pocket and spent it all on ice cream.

After his discharge, they moved back to Bemidji where Jim, courtesy of the GI bill, graduated from Bemidji Teacher's College with a teaching degree in history and physical education.  He fondly recalls Dr. Myrtle Hunt teaching him ballroom dance.  Jim worked at Nash Finch during college, played golf for Bemidji State, played on the city champion curling team and raised his growing family.  Jill and Jimmy arrived 18 months apart and Nash Finch covered both doctor and hospital bills.  That work ethic followed him throughout his life including his teaching and coaching career where, "I gave it my all."

Coach Musburger's players frequently drive to Bemidji to share memories and often send letters.  David Henry, '66 team member and retired air controller at O'Hare Airport, wrote: *Playing football and basketball under your guidance had a significant impact on my life and career.  You welcomed me to the team.  You encouraged me to work hard.  You demanded sportsmanship and good conduct.  The experience of that time prepared me for my career and my life.  The sense of team, hard work and good conduct allowed me to be successful and to share the values I learned from you with countless others.  Thanks for keeping me on the good path.*

My father shared stories with us over the years, always positive and full of humor.  One of my best memories growing up was the morning after a basketball game.  Dad would replay the entire game with me.  I felt special and valued that he shared his excitement with a teenage daughter.  Now it's time for his players and coaches to share their stores.  I was not prepared for the outpouring of affection, respect and devotion for Coach Musburger.  Not many of us experience this intense esteem and veneration from others.  Randy Hultgren, '76, repeated the sentiment expressed by other athletes over and over, *"I would have walked through a wall for Coach Musburger."*

# 1. ARRIVAL IN STRANDQUIST, AUGUST 1956

## *"A Polish Team from a Swedish Town with a German Coach"* –
KNOX-TV Grand Forks

In 1956, Jim Musburger was offered his first teaching and coaching job in Strandquist, a town with just over 100 residents, for the princely sum of $3000 a year.  The family of four packed up their meager belongings in Bemidji and headed north to the small Swedish and Polish settlement just an hour from the Canadian border.  They rented a house across the street from the school for $50 month.  Strandquist boasted a busy Main Street lined with the post office, Nelson's General Merchandise, Hansen's Food Market, Boen's Café, Carl Johnson's Oil & Gas station and Minnie's Café, where you could buy Sunday dinner for a dollar.  Other businesses included Bill Warde's Income Tax Service, Massey Harris S&S Implement Co., the Strandquist Co-op Elevator, City Hall, Les & Tony's Tavern, Swanson's Tavern, Strandquist Shipping Association, Ray Anderson's Strandquist Produce, Hougard's Sales & Service, Leo Renstrom's Garage & Repair Shop, Ted Kimbrough's Welding Shop (with an old race car in the back of the shop), Ed Stennes' barbershop, the school and two churches; St. Edward's Catholic Church and Bethesda Lutheran Church.

The community welcomed the young family with open arms and they became fast friends with Eddie and Marcy Nelson, who managed the general store on Main Street.  Sylvester and Clara Kasprowicz frequently invited them for Sunday dinner at their farm, and the kids learned how to climb a hayloft and navigate around cow pies.

Along with teaching history, physical education and science, Jim served as high school principal under Superintendent Leon Orcutt.  He also coached the Strandquist Warriors for five years without a losing season and took the team to the district finals twice.  KNOX TV in Grand Forks honored the Warriors as "Team of the Week" and named them the *"Polish team from a Swedish town with a German coach."*  Musburger also started the Letterman's Club and a baseball program in Strandquist, although he had only played sandlot ball.

**New Strandquist School 1960 after the January fire 1959**

### Strandquist School Song

*Strandquist High School, hats off to thee,*
*Firm and strong united we will ever be,*
*Strandquist High School hats off to thee.*
*Rah, rah, rah, rah, rah,*
*Rah, rah, rah, rah, rah,*
*Hats off to Strandquist High.*
("Minnesota Rouser")

## 2. STRANDQUIST WARRIORS 1956-57

*Coach Musburger made us work really hard and told us, "The way you practice is the way you will play." Every boy in the school went out for basketball except for two and they ended up the team managers.* – Donnie Carlson '57

Jim Musburger replaced Principal Roy Kerwin as Strandquist basketball coach in 1956. Basketball was the only school sport and like most small towns, the school was the social center of the farming community. That year, Strandquist enrolled ten seniors, eleven juniors, ten sophomores and eleven freshmen in the high school. Of the 42 students, 27 were boys. Despite the low numbers, the 1956-57 Warriors basketball team fielded a full roster including seniors Chester "Chet" Boen (co-captain), Wesley Vagle, and twin brothers Donnie (co-captain) and Ronnie Carlson. Juniors Richard Wikstrom, Francis Anderson, Paul Lindstrom and sophomores Jerry Carlson (brother of Donnie and Ronnie), Jimmy Larson and Robert "Red" Blazejewski filled out the team. David Kasprowicz and James Kline managed the team.

The Warriors defeated Middle River for their first win of the season and toppled Argyle in the first round of the sub-district on a desperation shot by Don Carlson to win 40-39. The season ended with ten wins and ten losses, a respectable record as the Warriors had not won a game the previous year. Jimmy Larson led the season scoring with 283 points followed by Donnie Carlson's 165 points and Chet Boen's 164 points.

In conference play, the Warriors defeated Middle River 50-36, Lake Bronson 54-52, Stephen 48-39, Lancaster 49-32, Newfolden 63-49, Karlstad 44-38, Lake Bronson 63-47, Alvarado 53-48 and Newfolden 58-42. The Warriors lost to Stephen 38-30, Argyle 56-46, Kennedy 74-40, Hallock 39-33, Karlstad 37-32, Argyle 58-48, Kennedy 67-46 and Hallock 58-49.

Varsity cheerleaders were Beverly Berggren, Betty Kasprowicz, Grace Larson and Caroline Stennes.

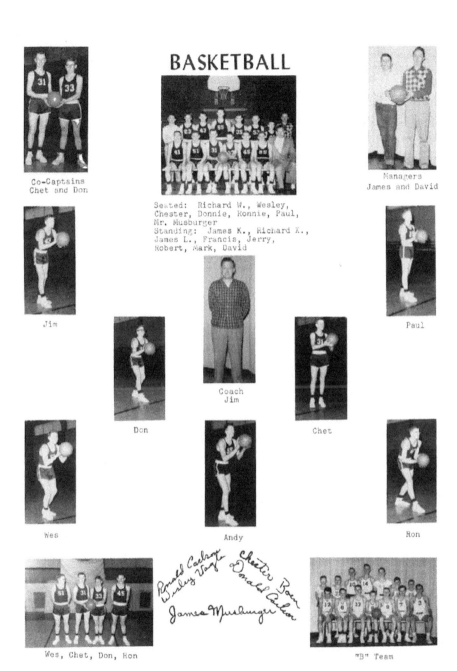

# BASKETBALL

Co-Captains
Chet and Don

Managers
James and David

Seated: Richard W., Wesley,
Chester, Donnie, Ronnie, Paul,
Mr. Musburger
Standing: James K., Richard K.,
James L., Francis, Jerry,
Robert, Mark, David

Jim

Paul

Coach
Jim

Don

Chet

Wes

Andy

Ron

Wes, Chet, Don, Ron

"B" Team

(1957 Strandquist Warrior)

**Donnie Carlson '57** tells how basketball changed the first year Jim Musburger coached in Strandquist: *Our previous coach would throw out a basketball, tell us to practice, and then leave for a cup of coffee downtown. When Mr. Musburger arrived in town, he took control and taught us how to play basketball. He made us work really hard and told us, "The way you practice is the way you will play." Every boy in the school went out for basketball except for two, and they ended up the team managers. After the first win, we knew we could win, and after the second win, the town was behind us all the way. Chet was left-handed and I was right-handed so we could shoot from both sides of the court. When we defeated Argyle in the sub-district on a last second desperation shot by me as the buzzer went off, our team gathered in the locker room and just hugged each other. This win was a dream come true. Coach made us believe in ourselves. We even beat Newfolden once that year and both Ron Ueland, who later coached for Newfolden, and Bobby Dahl, with his great hook shot, played on that good Newfolden team.*

*When Coach Musburger started the "S" Letterman's Club, we were so proud to wear our sweaters with the chevrons and letters. We served potato dumpling dinners to earn money for the state basketball tournament and the whole town turned out to support us. Mr. Musburger drove the four seniors in his Ford station wagon down to Williams Arena in the cities. We all wondered how many hay bales you could put in an arena that big! My dad was the school janitor and my mom worked as the school cook, so I couldn't get away with anything. My dad would let us in the gym on Saturday and Sunday to practice basketball on the pretense that we were helping him. There were only three television sets in the community so we were happy to play ball.*

 Eleven members qualified for membership in the first Letterman's Club, and they elected Doug Wikstrom president and Ronnie Carlson secretary-treasurer.

Whenever he had the chance, Strandquist student Allen Rasmussen would head to the back room of Johnson's gas station where a television set held center court surrounded by old, beat-up couches. This rare and highly prized technological wonder drew old and young alike to watch programs like "The $64,000 Question," and "What's My Line?"

Teammate **Chet Boen '57** echoes Donnie's memories: *Our senior year was the first year that Coach Musburger arrived in Strandquist and it was the first year we got to play in the new gym. Prior to this, we would run to the town hall to practice and play our home games. It was a really exciting time for us, both a new facility and a new coach! We knew that he came from Bemidji and had played for Bun Fortier's Lumberjacks and they always won the region and went to state. There was only one class back then. As Donnie said, "Musburger taught us how to play basketball."*

*One of the drills introduced to us early on was the 5-man weave. I didn't realize it until I started to coach myself, but this drill teaches pivoting, proper screening, movement without the ball, use of your off hand, protecting the ball and more. I remember we used it in our first game that year against Middle River at home. As we ran through this weave about five times, I think we put the Skippers to sleep, and I saw the middle wide open and took the rock to the hole and scored. Basketball was about the only sport in Strandquist mainly because of the number of students to participate; there were only five boys in our class of '57.*

*One game that really sticks out for me was against the Hallock Bears on Hallock's floor. We ended up upsetting them, but a snowstorm developed and they wouldn't let anyone leave the gym until it subsided. We got to celebrate in our opponent's own gym for about five hours before we could leave for home.*

*The state tournament trip was the icing on the cake for us. We raised money and I don't remember how many went to the big dance in the city, but it was a two-day trip. We stayed in Bemidji the first night and once we arrived in the cities, we stayed at the old Andrews Hotel on Hennepin Avenue. It was fun to see some of the small schools hold their own against Edina, Austin and Duluth. Many of us had never been to a city bigger than Grand Forks!*

*Yes, they were the best of times, and Coach Musburger was the reason for making our last year so enjoyable. Donnie and Ronnie Carlson and I went on to Bemidji State, and I came back to teach and coach B team basketball at Strandquist for five years. Musburger had been enticed away by our archrivals, the Karlstad Rabbits, when I arrived and it would have been so neat to be his assistant. Jim Musburger's approach to coaching was know the game, be firm, demand excellence, but most of all, have fun.*

Basketball practices were not taken lightly, and you were expected to perform at a consistently high level. Underclassman **Rodney Stromlund** tells about a funny incident: *Jim Musburger was my coach when we moved back to Minnesota from Arkansas. He was a great guy but I sure got on his bad list one day during basketball practice when I missed an easy shot that I normally would make. He told me as* *punishment to go down to the other end of the gym and keep shooting until he told me to stop. The practice ended and everyone went to the locker room except me. I was still shooting baskets out of spite so that he would have to tell me to stop. He read my mind perfectly and it aggravated him, so he told me to stop and threw a basketball at me. I jumped aside and it went straight to the bleachers where some girls were polishing white basketball shoes for the game that evening. He scored a perfect hit on the white polish bottle sending white shoe polish on the girls, the bleacher and the wall. I exited very quickly to the shower room. The next day everything was back to normal.*

**Wes Vagle '57** went out for the team his senior year: *I was not one of Coach Musburger's star athletes as I did not go out for basketball until my senior year. I would go in from time to time as a sub. Coach was always careful to put all of us on the second team in for a time nearly every game. The best thing about Coach Musburger was that he always took time for all of us. He made us feel good about ourselves and glad to be on the team. He was a real friend.*

(1961 Strandquist Warrior)

# 3. STRANDQUIST WARRIORS 1957-58

*Mr. Musburger would invite the basketball team to his home on a few Friday nights for ice cream. It seemed he intended his team would have a team social, then be sent home to get a good night's sleep and be refreshed for the game the next night. They guys on the team had other plans – head to Greenbush for the dance! –*
Pistol Pete Kasprowicz '61

The Warriors continued their winning record in 1957-58. They placed 3rd in the conference with a 12-4 record, topped by Hallock and Stephen. Varsity basketball players included Jerry Carlson, Jimmy Larson, Donny "Jeep" Larson, Francis Anderson (co-captain), Roger Kasprowicz, Paul Lindstrom, (co-captain) Jerry Szczepanski, Jerry Blaze, Pete Kasprowicz, brothers Richard and Doug Wikstrom and manager James Kline. Varsity cheerleaders were Kay Hahn, Carol Holmstrom, June Kleinwachter and Eileen Hanson.

1957-58 Strandquist Warriors: Front row: J. Kline, J. Larson, R. Wikstrom, P. Lindstrom, F. Anderson, G. Carlson, R. Blazejewski, Mr. Musburger. Back row: Mr. Orcutt, J. Szczepanski, P. Kasprowicz, R. Kasprowicz, R. Lundstrom, D. Wikstrom, R. Stennes, Mr. Waterworth. (1958 Strandquist Warrior)

The Warriors took 2nd place in the West Sub-District Tournament by eliminating Argyle 69-56 and Kennedy 58-52, before losing a heart stopper to Stephen 60-57. During District 32 Tournament play, Strandquist Warrior Jimmy Larson scored 19 points to edge the Baudette Bears 49-48, but the Warriors could not stop Hallock's Neil Bengtson and lost in the semi-finals 77-45. In the consolation round, the Warriors rebounded by defeating Kennedy in overtime 64-63 for third place. Jerry Carlson led the scoring with 23 points. The *Middle River Record* reported: *This group represents one of the finest basketball teams to ever play for the Warriors. They're small, but good shots, good ball handlers and fast.* (files of Jerry Szczepanski)

**The three seniors of the Strandquist Warrior basketball team accepted the trophy from tournament manager Superintendent Sonju of Kennedy last Friday night when Strandquist took second place in the West Sub-district tournament. On the left is Francis Anderson, Strandquist's biggest boy. Next to him is Richard Wikstrom, the little tricky playmaker, and Paul Lindstrom, who is an accurate shot from out on the floor.**
(6 March 1958, *Karlstad Advocate*)

**Connie Lubarski's** cousins played on the Strandquist team: *Coach Musburger was in Strandquist for most of my elementary school days. I remember watching Musburger coached teams with Francis Anderson, the Wikstroms, Donnie Carlson, my cousins the Kasprowicz brothers, Roger (Big Moose) and Richard (Little Moose), and also Pistol Pete Kasprowicz. They were awesome. They were my heroes. It was said that Jim left for Karlstad after the three Kasprowicz boys graduated. Coach Musburger went to Karlstad and a year later the land on our farm by Florian was annexed to the Argyle School District. So in the fall of 1963, we were in Argyle. My parents had the restaurant, Mary and Ed's Café, in Strandquist for a while and the motto was, "If you want to get fed, go to Mary and Ed." It was always great to have the players and Coach Musburger come in there. Jim Musburger was someone special to our family. There was always respect and a bit of awe in his presence.*

Strandquist lost and Argyle won when Lubarski's farm was annexed to their school district in 1963. Conrad was an all-conference basketball player for Argyle High School in '67, '68, and '69. His brother, Richard, also played on the '67 basketball team, and his younger brother, Greg, played football and basketball from 1976-80.

Conrad coached the Argyle High School football team from 1977-1983. His teams took first place in eleven-man football in '77, '78, '79 and in nine-man starting in 1980. They also claimed the conference championship or a share of the championship the next four years in Top of the State Conference. In 1980, the Eagles lost in first round play to qualify for the state playoffs, but in 1981, they went undefeated (13-0) and won the Nine Man Football State Championship, the first state championship for any small school in northwestern Minnesota. During his last two years of coaching, Argyle lost in the state semi-finals in 1982 and in the quarter-finals in 1983. Coach Lubarski was named Conference Coach of the Year in '80, '81, '82, and '83, and State Nine-Man Coach of the Year in 1981.

Ironically, Conrad played football only his senior year: *We had farm work in the fall and helped our neighbors dig potatoes. Our potato digging money was for clothes and spending money during the basketball season.*

# 4. STRANDQUIST WARRIORS 1958-59

*Strandquist had some excellent athletes during Musburger's tenure: the Carlsons, Kasprowiczs, Jimmy Larson (one of the area's best), Doug Wikstrom and Bobby Stennes.* - Ron Ueland '61, Newfolden

On January 31, 1959, one of the coldest nights of the year, tragedy hit the community when defective wiring on the first floor of the school started a fire that burned down the entire school except for the new gymnasium. Everything was lost in the building and the $350,000 loss was initially believed to be only partially covered by $155,000 in insurance. Following the fire the basketball team practiced once again in the town hall as classes were held in the gymnasium. Coach Musburger recalls sweeping up all the beer caps on Monday morning in the town hall after the dance on Saturday night.

But the loss of their school did not stop the talented Warriors as they continued their court success in 1958-59. The season opened with a thrilling victory over Baudette 51-50 and ended with 18 wins and 6 losses when the team tipped Lancaster 60-59. The Grand Forks KNOX-TV "Team of the Week" roster consisted of co-captains Jerry Carlson and Jim Larson, Robert Blazejewski; Roger Kasprowicz, Richard "Dick" Kasprowicz, Robert Stennes, Doug Wikstrom, Donald Larson, Robert Kline, Gus Berggren, Richard "Pete" Kasprowicz and Merrill Stennes. Wallace Hanson and Larry Adlis served as team managers. Along with his "Team of the Week," Coach Jim Musburger won honors as "Coach of the Week," and Jim Larson was named "Player of the Week." Coach Musburger and Mr. Frank, the Industrial Arts teacher, drove the whole team in two cars to Grand Forks to appear on television.

Conference season wins included: Baudette 51-50, Middle River 62-42, Argyle 60-41, Humboldt 58-32, Stephen 65-63, Karlstad 58-31, Kennedy 64-57, Humboldt 69-30, Lake Bronson 66-51, Argyle 73-60, Karlstad 63-55, Hallock 62-49, Lancaster 60-59. The Warriors lost to: Lancaster, 62-43, Lake Bronson 59-57 and Stephen 86-73. At the Karlstad Christmas Tournament, Strandquist topped Karlstad 58-39 and Newfolden tipped Strandquist 47-46.

To top off a great conference record, the Warriors won the Sub-District championship by defeating Humboldt 77-45, Lancaster 58-56 and Stephen 57-53 at Hallock. They took third place in the district by nudging Baudette 53-51, lost to Lancaster 76-57, and defeated Stephen 59-58. Jimmy Larson led the season scoring with 495 points followed by Jerry Carlson with 362, Robert Blazejewski with 156, Pete Kasprowicz with 147, and Roger Kasprowicz with 113 points.

When Strandquist defeated the highly-ranked Hallock Bears during conference play, Coach Musburger shared the story that the Hallock coach, who wrote all his plays on a small handheld blackboard, broke his blackboard in half!

**1958-59 Strandquist Warriors: Record 18-6: Front row: Gene Berggren, Pete Kasprowicz, Robert Blazejewski, James Larson, Gerald Carlson, Douglas Wikstrom, Donald Larson. Back row: Coach Musburger, Gerald Blaze, Richard Kasprowicz, Robert Kasprowicz, Robert Kline, Robert Stennes**
(1959 Strandquist Warrior)

**Richard "Pistol Pete" Kasprowicz '61** wrote about the fire:  *I do remember we were bused to Karlstad's gym after school for basketball practice when Strandquist's school burned down.  The school was in the process of canceling its present insurance policy and getting a new policy.  During this transition, the school burned down.  The school district was able to collect on both policies.  I don't think this could be done today!*

*Because the school was totally destroyed, the state wanted to close the school.  The school superintendent went to Minneapolis and argued the case against closing.  As a result, the school was rebuilt.  Because of the two policies, the school was totally paid for, no debt on the taxpayers.*

**Betty Kasprowicz '59**, Pete's sister, was a cheerleader that year:  *The fire was horrible – I watched the school burn from our farmhouse kitchen window.  I lost a camera in the fire, a Christmas gift from a good friend.  Our new cheerleading uniforms burned in the fire so we ended the year wearing our white sweaters with the big "S" on the front and black slacks.  As seniors, we had saved enough money to take a class trip to Yellowstone National Park, but the majority of our funds were lost in the fire, so we went to Canada instead.*

**Varsity cheerleaders 1959:  Anna Chwialkowski, Janice Larson, Marlys Brekke, Betty Kasprowicz and Eileen Hanson.**
(1959 Strandquist Warrior)

25

**1959 Strandquist Sub-District champions**
( 4 March 1959, *Middle River Record*)

Newfolden player and coach **Ron Ueland '61** offers sports history in District 32: *During the 30 years after World War II and before the advent of girls sports in the mid 70's, boys basketball dominated life in small town Northwest Minnesota. For two weeks in March during tournaments, it became the center of the universe. The players and coaches were central figures in the community, much respected, sometimes revered. Newfolden had such a coach in Jack Junker, Strandquist had Jim Musburger.*

*Prior to the advent of a class system for Minnesota basketball tournaments, District 32 was unique in that there were no big schools like Bemidji, Crookston or Thief River Falls. The biggest schools, Warroad, Roseau, Baudette and Hallock, all had hockey to compete for their top athletes. As a result, District 32 had only one Region champ,*

*Roseau in 1946, and a different champion every year. The tournament was incredibly exciting.*

*While I attended high school in Newfolden 1957-61, Jim Musburger coached in Strandquist. Though we didn't know much about neighboring coaches, we all knew about Jim Musburger ten miles to the north in Strandquist. Admittedly, Strandquist had some excellent athletes during his tenure: the Carlson boys, Kasprowicz boys, Jimmy Larson (one of the area's best), Doug Wikstrom and Bobby Stennes. Our '59 team won the district. We beat Strandquist 47-46 during the regular season. Strandquist finished third in the district tournament.*

*In 1960, when I was a junior, we met Strandquist in the quarter finals of the district tournament and Strandquist won by 8 points. It seemed worse. It was my first experience playing against Musburger's daunting defense. I remember it being a very frustrating night. In '61, we won close games against Strandquist 39-34 and 32-31 in the old Soo Line Tournament. Though Strandquist was one of the smallest schools in old District 32 during the Musburger era, they were one of the best and we always had a lot of respect for them.*

**Strandquist Lettermen's Club April 1959: Front row: Don Larson, Robert "Red" Blazejewski, Jerry Carlson. Back row: Jerry Blaze, Robert Stennes, Doug Wikstrom, Roger Kasprowicz, Richard "Pete" Kasprowicz, Allen Rasmussen, Jerry Szczepanski, Robert Kline.** (1959 Strandquist Warrior)

# DEDICATION

We, the Senior Class of 1959, wish to express our appreciation for the advice and guidance we received from our principal and class advisor, Mr. Musburger, through the dedication of our annual, The Warrior of 1959. (1959 Strandquist Warrior)

Strandquist High School
CLASS of 1959

Marlene Rud — Leon M Orcutt, Supt. — J.H. Musburger, Princ. — Joyce Adlis

Gerald Carlson — Marie Kleinvachter — JoAnne Chwialkowski — James Larson

Robert Blazejewski — Harriet Hanson — Marlys Brekke — Betty Kasprowicz

Cooper Studio

# -1959-

Leon M. Orcutt, Supt.     J.H. Musburger,
Princ.     Marlene Rud     Joyce Adlis
Gerald Carlson     Marie Kleinvachter
JoAnn Chwialkowski     James Larson
Robert Blazejewski     Harriet Hanson
Marlys Brekke     Betty Kasprowicz

## 5. STRANDQUIST WARRIORS 1959-60

*We were playing in the Christmas tournament at Strandquist, and I was taking the ball out of bounds. The fans sat on the bleachers, which were right next to us. All of a sudden, I felt someone brush my leg. A fan seated on the lowest bleacher had a heart attack, fell off the bleacher and died later at the Karlstad hospital. The officials stopped the game briefly, and they carried him out the side door of the gym and the game went on.* – Allen Rasmussen'61

**1959-60 Strandquist Warriors: Front row: Allen Rasmussen, Douglas Wikstrom, Richard "Pete" Kasprowicz, Roger Kasprowicz, Richard Kasprowicz, Robert Stennes. Back row: Larry Adlis, Jerry Szczepanski, James Stallock, Robert Kline, Jerry Blaze, Don Larson, James Dziengel.** (1960 Strandquist Warrior)

In 1959 -1960, the Varsity basketball team, led by seniors Roger Kasprowicz and Robert Kline, included juniors Allen Rasmussen, Doug Wikstrom, Pete Kasprowicz, Robert Stennes, Jerry Szczepanski and Jerry Blaze; sophomores James Stallock, Donny Larson, Dick Kasprowicz, and managers Larry Adlis and James Dziengel. This talented and feisty basketball team posted a season record 10-8, placed third in the sub-districts and advanced to the district championship game where they faced a tough Argyle team that beat them by one point, 43-42. Richard Kasprowicz ate a bag of peanuts at half time, got sick, and that lousy bag of nuts cost them the game.

Excited and proud Strandquist students wrote a weekly account of the basketball team in the *Middle River Record* during March 1960.

**March 9, 1960**: Readers, this has been a full packed week of activities for us. Basketball and more basketball. First of all, we played Newfolden last Friday night and ended up on the short end by a score of 51-44. Our boys played a terrific game, but because of the small floor space, they couldn't click the way they should. This game ended the 1959-60 basketball season. Our record for the season was 10 wins and 5 losses. This year the sub-district is held in Kennedy. The first round was played last night and the results are: Hallock beat Kennedy and we beat Lake Bronson 44-39. Let's keep the good work up, boys, and win them all. We are having a hard time doing our school work because of the basketball tournament. We ended our sub-district tournament by winning Lancaster for third place and received a very nice trophy.

**March 16, 1960**: We are happy to win the third place trophy in the sub-district tournament. By taking this honor, we have a place in the district tournament which is played in Hallock. So far we have done exceptionally well and tomorrow night we are playing in the finals against Argyle. The winner of this game wins the district title and will participate in the regional which is held in the Grand Forks Fieldhouse.

**March 23, 1960**: We are happy that we won second place in the district basketball tournament played last night in Hallock. It was a close game with Strandquist ending up 42-43.

**March 30, 1960**: The basketball team would sincerely like to thank the American Legion and all persons who so generously contributed to sending the team to the State Basketball Tournament.

**Pete Kasprowicz** reminisces: *We sold tickets to a potato pancake and sausage meal to raise money to travel to Minneapolis for the state* *tournament. The team stayed two nights in a hotel, the first experience for most of us. We had to put in a quarter to watch the television.*

**Varsity Cheerleaders: Anna Chwialkowski, Shirley Wigen, Janice Larson, Kathy Chwialkowski, Carol Holmstrom**
(1960 Strandquist Warrior)

Athletic eligibility rules were strictly enforced. At the beginning of the basketball season, the parents of every student signing up to play basketball received a letter outlining athletic eligibility rules and a sportsman's creed: *Sportsmanship is something that you cannot steal or buy...Because it is the product of how hard you really try... It is the spirit of the heart... you put into a game... to play it fair without regard... For any claim to fame... It is the emblem of your soul... As you are real sincere... in striving to be worthy of... Each handshake and each cheer... And more important, the strength... To take it standing up... When you feel sure you should have won... A medal or a cup... Sportsmanship is honest play... And taking things in stride... As you perform your best, so God... is always at your side.*

STRANDQUIST HIGH SCHOOL
INDEPENDENT DIST. 444
STRANDQUIST, MINNESOTA

October, 1960

Dear Parent:

As basketball season is about to begin once again,
it is a pleasure to have your son (or sons) _____
Jerry Szczepanski as a member of the Strandquist
Basketball Team.

As you know, we here at Strandquist High School,
have established a tradition in athletics of clean
living and sportsmanship. In order to maintain this high
standard, training rules must be made and enforced
throughout the coming school year. Besides, the rules
below, I would appreciate your cooperation in seeing that
your son receives the best possible diet to insure his
health.

Rules:

1. Absolutely no smoking. ( removal for three weeks)

2. Absolutely no use of alcoholic beverages. (removal for year

3. Curfew: 10:00 P.M. weekdays (Sunday included)
            11:30 P.M. Saturday night
            (removal for three weeks)
            (second offense, remainder of year)

4. Passing of subjects in school in order to maintain
   elegibility. (removal for six weeks)

I know that I can count on your cooperation during
the coming year, and I look forward to seeing you at
our events.

Sincerely,

James Musburger
James Musburger
Coach

# 6. STRANDQUIST WARRIORS 1960-61

*It will be a hot time in the old town tonight!* --Strandquist
Superintendent Leon Orcutt, collecting admission money at home
basketball games

Coach Musburger coached his final Strandquist basketball team in
1960-61. Team players Doug Wikstrom, Allen Rasmussen, Don
Larson, David Thompson, Jerry Blaze, Wallace Hanson, Richard
Kasprowicz, Pete Kasprowicz, Jerry Szczepanski, Joseph
Budziszewski, Eugene Kleinwachter, Jimmy Stallock and managers
Larry Adlis and James Dziengel, boasted a 13 - 6 record, including
three games won or lost by one point.

**Front row: J. Dziengel and L. Adlis. Back row left to right: D.
Larson, J. Budziszewski, W. Hanson, D. Wikstrom, J. Szczepanski,
R. Kasprowicz, P. Kasprowicz, D. Thompson, E. Kleinwachter, J.
Blaze, A. Rasmussen. Missing: J. Stallock**
(1961 Strandquist Warrior)

At the beginning of the season, **Coach Jim Musburger** commented: *With only one man over six feet tall, it is going to be a struggle for Strandquist this year. Though we have four regulars back, we lack depth. Our shooting will be a serious problem. Last year we averaged around 40 points a game. I feel that all of the teams in the Northern Lights Conference are respectable. Lake Bronson, Hallock and Argyle would have to be given consideration for the title.* (*Middle River Record*, from the files of Jerry Szczepanski)

The talented team topped Karlstad, Kennedy, Lake Bronson and Lancaster before losing to Newfolden 32-31 and Lake Bronson 41-35. They trounced Stephen 56-21 and tipped Argyle 51-50 before falling to Hallock 47-42. Humboldt went down 50-27 and Karlstad fell 51-45 before Lake Bronson squeaked by with a 53-49 victory. Lancaster and Stephen fell next followed by losses to Newfolden 39-34 and Argyle 62-58. The Warriors finished the regular season with victories over Baudette 50-47 and Middle River 61-43. Kennedy upset the Warriors in the first round of sub-district play 64-56 to end the season.

**Pistol Pete Kasprowicz '61** earned a unique nickname: *Mr. Musburger said I was one of his players who could consistently shoot a basket from mid court, today called a 3-pointer. He said if this 3-point rule was in effect then, we would have won more games. This is why I got the nickname "Pistol-Pete" from Mr. Musburger. And the name stuck.*

*Mr. Musburger was my history teacher, probably everyone's favorite teacher. He taught us about World War II and Pearl Harbor, never realizing I would join the US Navy after graduation and be stationed at Pearl Harbor for four years. I came home as a Vietnam Veteran.*

**Coach Musburger** added: *Pistol Pete had an unorthodox shot from the lower right side. The Argyle coach asked, "My God, how does he do it?" I replied, I'm not going to change it.*

**Varsity Cheerleaders: Betty Berggren, Kathy Chwialkowski, Ina Lou Nelson, June Kleinwachter, Carol Holmstrom and Eileen Hanson.** (1961 Strandquist Warrior)

Religion played a huge part in small towns, and Strandquist was no exception. Many of the athletes, including **Allen Rasmussen '61**, belonged to conservative churches, which looked down on sports. Allen's minister refused to let the boys play basketball, as he believed the sport was too loud and rowdy, not a good environment for Christians. However, he was allowed to play in the pep band on one condition – they had to leave at half time to avoid the raucous crowds. Allen lucked out when a new minister arrived in town: *I pled my case that the team did not have enough players and the minister agreed, and I played basketball my junior and senior year.* His parents never attended basketball games but they would listen to Doug Tegtmeier's broadcast on KTRF Radio in Thief River Falls.

```
       POTATO DUMPLING SUPPER

Wednesday, February 22, 1961

Strandquist School Cafeteria

5:30 p.m. - 8:30 p.m.

Price- Adults 75¢
       School Children 50¢
       Preschool 35¢
```

Allen recalls the rifle raffle and the pancake and Polish sausage suppers put on by the Letterman's Club (cooked by Clara Kasprowicz and Jeanette Carlson in the school cafeteria) to pay for their annual trip to the state tournament. Ironically, a Karlstad basketball referee, Palmer Oistad, won the rifle drawing two years in a row. In an era without activity buses, the coach (and one year, athlete Bob Stennes), drove the team to the cities. Allen also remembers that Adeline, the coach's wife, would host the team for barbecues and hot dogs at their home when she wasn't busy washing their uniforms.

NAME _____

ADDRESS _____

50¢ EACH       THREE FOR $1.00
Donation to Strandquist "S" Club
Holder of this ticket is entitled
to an equal chance on drawing for
30 - 30 MARLIN RIFLE
Drawing to be held
WED., NOVEMBER 9, 1960
Winner need not be present

Allen vividly recalls his first basketball game: *My first game out of town was in Baudette. We would eat poached eggs and toast or Swiss steak in the school cafeteria before we left for a game, as coach believed it would not upset our stomachs. Baudette had a great team that year and a great player named Nielsen. Coach put me in at the end of the game and I stole the ball, but got so excited that I missed the shot.* Allen was determined to attend all basketball practices: *We had practice over Christmas vacation and we lived 3 ½ miles out of town. I had to drive the tractor to town as my folks had the car. It was damn cold!*

**Jerry Szczepanski '61** made varsity his junior year: *We ran laps endlessly around the gym and I lapped everyone twice. Eating was very important to the coach and we held contests to see who could eat the most tuna milk sandwiches.*

Although Jim Musburger had played only sandlot baseball, he started a baseball team in Strandquist in 1958. Unlike basketball, Allen was allowed to play baseball his freshman year because the environment was less rowdy (outside) and his father liked baseball. The school board voted to buy uniforms and equipment and in 1961, eleven young men filled the roster: Co-captains Allen Rasmussen and Jerry Szczepanski, Richard Thompson, Pete Kasprowicz, David

Chwialkowski, Dennis Chwialkowski, James Dziengel, Wallace Hanson, Joseph Budziszewski, Dick Kasprowicz and Dennis Kasprowicz. Musburger remembers calling plays for the team using numbers until during one game, Captain Rasmussen, who Coach called a smart kid, said, *"Coach, you don't have to call out the numbers anymore, we know them."*

**Baseball captains Jerry Szczepanski and Allen Rasmussen**
(1961 Strandquist Warrior)

Newfolden's **Ron Ueland '61**recalls playing baseball against a Musburger coached Strandquist team:  *There are two things I distinctly remember about one game against Strandquist. Jimmy Larson hit a massive homerun, and later I was benched because I made an error by missing a throw from the catcher at second base.  I was a good hitter* *but a weak outfielder, so my coach told me that I better get a lot of hits because my fielding skills were so poor.*

**Strandquist Warriors Baseball Team 1961**
(1961 Strandquist Warrior)

Allen tells another funny story:  *Some of the Polish kids did not always come to school in the spring as they worked on the farm during planting season – this was a real problem for the baseball team as many of the players were Polish, and they were really good at baseball.  Most hailed from Florian, a small Polish settlement with a beautiful Catholic Church, the National Polish Alliance Hall and a baseball field.  Jerry Szczepanski's dad, Stanley, coached the Florian Falcons summer baseball team, and Coach Musburger depended on him and Charlie Krantz, the mailman, for coaching assistance.*

*Superintendent Orcutt loaned me his '58 Dodge to drive to the player's homes to convince the parents to let the kids play in the school baseball game. So I would drive out to the field, get the player off the tractor and take him to school for the game. When the Strandquist School closed in 1991, I gave the last commencement address, told this story, and ended the speech, "We were the only baseball team that showered before the game."*

Allen graduated from college and continued his career in education as High School superintendent, and later, President of Rainy River College, both in International Falls, Minnesota: *Coach Musburger was my idol, my mentor and my inspiration to attend college and become an educator . I owe whatever success I had in life and my career in education largely to his example and encouragement. During my career, I always remembered Coach Musburger's advice, "Always be prepared for your next move, get yourself in position, you may not get the ball every time, but when you do, you can make a good pass or take a good shot.*

*It is the same in life.*

# -1961-

Mr. James H. Musburger, Prin.    Mr.
Leon M. Orcutt, Supt.    Robert Stennes
Shirley Berggren    Ronald Donarski
Carol Banaszewski    Richard A.
Kasprowicz    Shirley Chwialkowski
Jerry Blaze    Joan Kleinvachter    Jerry
Szczepanski    June Kleinvachter    Anna
Chwialkowski    Allen Rasmussen
Camilla Newman    Eileen Hanson
Douglas Wikstrom    Ina Lou Nelson

(1961 Strandquist Warrior)

# FRIENDLY ENEMIES

Watching them on the bench, one would almost think Jim and Wally were the worst of enemies. Jim is Mr. Musburger, coach of the Strandquist Warriors, and Wally is Mr. Boen, the Rabbit tutor. Actually the two men are close friends and spend considerable time together, but they are similar in the fact that they live and die with their respective teams while they are in action. The two were on the floor simultaneously after the ball game here Friday night to shake each other's hand — and the handclasp is always sincere between these two battlers. If the picture of Jim on the left and Wally on the right is good enough, you can tell by the ruffled hair and sweat on their brows that they have both had a hard workout.

**Strandquist Warriors Coach Jim Musburger and his good friend and rival, Karlstad Rabbits Coach Wally Boen**
(2 February 1961 *Karlstad Advocate*)

# 7. HEADING NORTH TO KARLSTAD

In 1960, the Musburger family moved seven miles north to Karlstad for housing when their home in Strandquist sold. They rented Albert Grandstrand's house just across the road from the hospital, two blocks from the school and the gym, and most importantly for the kids, right next to the outdoor skating rink. The thriving small town on Highway 59 boasted a full main street: Mar-Pal Market, Erickson's Hartz, Mortenson's Food Market, Nordin Hotel and Restaurant, Karlsson's Swedish Hotel, Wally's Radio Service, Dave Seng's Theater, Winjum's Department Store, Berg Drug, The Karlstad Advocate, Karlstad State Bank, Wikstrom Telephone Company, Wikstrom Jewelers, Margaret Olsen's Coffee Shop, Jay's Barbershop, Trane & Celany Furniture, Porter's Tavern, Karlstad Auto Parts, Anderson's Phillip's 66, Carlson Sales Co., Carlson Oil Company, Skogerboe Clinic, Scherer's Dentistry, Standard Service Station, Netterlund Heating, Farmer's Elevator, Summers Fertilizer, Co-op Creamery, Anderson's Hardware, Parker Motors, Henry Peterson's Karlstad Auto Parts, The Beauty Spot and several churches.

Jim Musburger continued to teach and coach in Strandquist until the fall of 1961, when he traded in the Warriors Maroon and White for the Rabbits Blue and White. Musburger joined the teaching staff in Karlstad, where he taught history and physical education and served as assistant football and basketball coach under Wally Boen. He also coached the B basketball team and coached golf in the spring. Wally left at the end of the year and the school board asked Musburger to take on varsity basketball coaching duties, but he declined out of respect for his good friend, Wally. Ron Juell accepted the head football and basketball coaching positions and when he left a year later, Jim Musburger agreed to take the varsity basketball position the fall of 1964.

Coach Musburger took the team to a 7-11 record the first season and successfully mentored the team to competitive seasons for the next 19 years. He was also the assistant football coach and head golf coach during this time. Over the years, he won accolades and praise from competing coaches, referees and administration for his sportsmanship, excellent discipline and enviable record.

**Karlstad High School 1961**

## Karlstad School Song

*Karlstad High School stand up and cheer,*
*It's a loyal crowd that's here.*
*With a rah, rah, rah and a sis-boom-bah,*
*For the Karlstad team we cheer, rah, rah, rah.*
*Come on gang, on your toes slam-bang,*
*Hit 'em high and hit 'em low.*
*So fight, Karlstad High School fight,*
*Mighty Rabbits come on let's go!*
*R-A-B-B-I-T-S, yaaaaaaay, RABBITS!*
(tune – "Minnesota Fight Song")

# MR. JAMES MUSBURGER
## Social Studies
## Coach and Phy. Ed.

(1963 Karlstad Bluebook)

## 8. KARLSTAD RABBITS 1961-64: COACHING THE B TEAM

*Coach frequently said we should play for the fun of it, and would add, "It's no fun to lose."*– Neil Skogerboe '66

In 1961-62, Coach Jim Musburger began his Karlstad coaching career with the B basketball team. Players included Jim Johnson, Hollis Turnwall, Duane Undeberg, Dennis Anderson, Don Krantz, Loren Hams, Billy Struck, Neil Skogerboe, Neil Wikstrom and Brian Sjodin. The age of the players ranged from Brian in 7th grade to Don, a junior.

**Jim Johnson '65** recalls that year: *I was told not to expect much playing time as I could only go to practice once a week because I had to help on my parent's farm. I did make up for it as an adult by playing independent men's league basketball for 30 years!*

Karlstad B Team 1961-62
Kneeling: J. Johnson, H. Turnwall, D. Undeberg, D. Anderson, D. Krantz. Standing: L. Hams, B. Struck, N. Skogerboe, N. Wikstrom, B. Sjodin, Coach Musburger
(1962 Karlstad Bluebook)

# KARLSTAD B TEAM 1962-63

*I still ache when I think about all the work we put in at practice each day. But at game time, it all paid off.* - Glenn Pederson '66

**Neil Skogerboe '66** wrote about playing on Musburger's B team in 1962-63: *When I was in 9th grade, Mr. Musburger was our B team coach. He never made us run just to run, but we would do hours of various drills ending in layups. Some practices he kept us going and going and going. He did not appreciate taking it easy (loafing). We were in constant motion for at least half of the practice time. One practice he got after me for not being fully engaged. I was taken out of the starting lineup and had to play defense against them. I turned up the intensity, got many rebounds, blocked several shots, and intercepted a few passes. I probably committed a few fouls, but Mr. Musburger was grinning. He was a master of motivation. Once, when I was in 10th grade, our B team played against the A team. We beat them rather soundly. The Coach told us not to gloat or talk about it.*

Karlstad B Team 1962-63: Kneeling left to right: Ernie Pietruszewski, Troy Dagen, Glenn Pederson, Neil Skogerboe, Tom Folland, Loren Hams, Neil Wikstrom, Brian Sjodin, Allen Schmidt. Standing left to right: Jack Oistad, Skip Borneman, Mark McNelly, Barry Lund, Tim Nordin, David Henry, Gary Hultgren, Mark Erickson, Jeff Folland and Paul Bostrom.
(1963 Karlstad Bluebook)

# KARLSTAD B TEAM 1963-64

*When practice was planned, you tried to be there and once, in the middle of a snow storm when the roads closed, I took our snowcat ten miles to be part of it, you didn't want to miss practice and warm the bench.* – Troy Dagen '66

**Karlstad B Team 1963-64:  First row:  Jack Oistad, Allen Schmidt, David Henry, Tom Folland, Troy Dagen, Glenn Pederson, Skip Borneman.  Second row:  Bryce Anderson, manager, Greg Oistad, Tim Olson, Tim Nordin, Ernie Pietruszewski, Mark McNelly, Coach Jim Musburger** (1964 Karlstad Bluebook)

**Troy Dagen '66** remembers his earliest years playing basketball:  *Our career with Mr. Musburger started in the lower grades where we would all pile in a station wagon to play other towns moving up to C, B, and finally, A team, all the same players and our coach right with us.  We didn't have a tall team but were determined to be the best.  He wanted you to be a part of his team.  His beliefs and the A team's coach were not the same, so we would practice in the small gym and they in the big gym.  We would play the A team for practice beating them or giving them a run for their money.  When practice was planned, you tried to be there and once, in the middle of a snow storm when the roads closed, I took our snowmobile ten miles to be part of it, you didn't want to miss practice and warm the bench.  I think all the players had the same* *attitude. That was why we had a good last year by all the years playing together with a coach that wanted us to play our best and be the best.*

**Tim Olson '67** moved back to Karlstad in 9th grade: *When I was a freshman at Karlstad, there was the B team and the A team. The B team had sophomores, freshmen, and one 8th grader, Brian Sjodin. The 8th grader was older than me by a month, but better by about ten years. He started on the B team when the season began, but soon moved up to the A team, where he started also. So by default I got to play quite a bit on the B team. And we had a pretty good B team. We used to say to ourselves that people would come to watch the B team play, and then leave. The A team won one game all year against Strandquist. In fact, there was a play-in game between Karlstad and Strandquist at the end of the regular season, where the winner would advance to the sub-district tournament. Strandquist won that game. We, as a B team, had a record of 13-3, and all three of our losses were very close. So Coach had good reason to just play his B team and Brian next year when he took over as varsity coach. I think that is why he decided to play without seniors and continue building his team.*

*I learned a lesson in the classroom that year, and this is my version of the desk tipping incident that everyone remembers. Our family moved from Karlstad to Roseau for two years, my 7th and 8th grades. Roseau kids had attitude, and I learned from them. When we moved back to Karlstad, I forgot to leave that in Roseau. It wasn't that I was disrespecting adults, more like I thought I was better than most of my classmates, sort of. I had a growth spurt, so when I started 9th grade, I was taller than a lot of my classmates. Anyway, that one day in civics class, we took a test where we had to write out answers to certain questions. Mr. Musburger had the class correct the papers, where he would give general answers to the question asked, and then we would have to decide if the answer on the sheet came close to the general answer or not. The first time I asked if Gayle's answer would pass, Musburger said it was close enough. I remember thinking that this answer wasn't even close and shook my head. A little while later, another abstract answer came up on the sheet I was checking, and I got the same answer from the teacher. I remember shaking my head again, like " I can't believe he is allowing this answer to pass," when all of a sudden the desk and I are both tipped over. Then the back of my collar*

*and I are carried out the door to the principal's office.  I
know Musburger once said that if anyone ever got kicked out of his
class, it "would take an act of Congress to get that person
reinstated."   Well, you know that was the best thing that could have
happened to me.  I lost that attitude really quick after that and never
got it back.  Mr. Musburger sure knew how to get someone's attention.
And as contrite as a puppy, I was allowed back in class.*

**B Team Cheerleaders:
Karen Stavenau, Peggy
Spilde, Virginia Olson**

**1964 Golf Team:  left to
right:  Ray Koland, Craig
Spilde, Don Krantz, Allen
Sjodin, Brian Sjodin, Jack
Oistad** (1964 Bluebook)

## 9. KARLSTAD RABBITS A TEAM 1964-65

*I remember one practice Neil Wikstrom and I were in line shooting layups and Neil said something to me that coach overheard. He came over to us and told both of us to go down to the locker room and not come back until we were ready to play. So we went down to the locker room, looked at each other, and ran right back up. –*
Brian Sjodin '68

In 1964-65, Coach Musburger accepted his first varsity coaching job in Karlstad. In an unprecedented move, he moved his entire B team to the varsity and played without a senior on the team. The season record was 7-11 and ended with a one-point victory, 34-33, over Strandquist, Musburger's former team. Playing only juniors, sophomores, and one freshman, Brian Sjodin, he was building a team.

Karlstad Varsity Basketball Team 1964-65: Seated: Paul Bostrom, manager, Troy Dagen, Neil Skogerboe, Brian Sjodin, Neil Wikstrom (captain), Ernie Pietruszewski, David Henry, Tim Olson, Mark Erickson, manager. Standing: Coach Musburger, Mark McNelly, Glenn Pederson, Ken Gorsuch, Tom Folland, Jack Oistad, Coach Heck. (1965 Karlstad Bluebook)

The Rabbits defeated Newfolden 50-47, Hallock 67-54, Humboldt 79-37, Kennedy 50-48, Humboldt 93-41, Greenbush 62-33 and Strandquist 34-33. Season losses included Sacred Heart 68-48, Lake Bronson 40-27, Stephen 73-58, Argyle 46-38, Lancaster 56-46, Strandquist 56-52, Lake Bronson 63-51, Stephen 88-59, Hallock 56-40, Argyle 49-46 and Lancaster 54-48.

**Glenn Pederson '66** recalls basketball practices: *Jim was like a drill sergeant when it came to conditioning. At the end of the school day, we met in the gym and we trained and ran scrimmages for about two hours. I recall he had us doing lots of wind sprints, running laps around the gym, and lots of 3-on-2 fast break drills. We did this for what seemed like forever. And after lots of practicing plays in scrimmage, we had more running and conditioning before we could hit the showers. Well, long story short, there was a "method to his madness." We were not a long team, our tallest player was about 6'1" and we needed to be able to apply a full-court press at any time, and just "out-hustle" the opposing team to win. Jim was all about winning, and so we had successful seasons due to his dedication to physical conditioning and learning fundamental basketball. I expect this is the way he learned basketball in Bemidji. I still ache when I think about all the work we put in at practice each day! But at game time, it all paid off. I also remember many of the offensive play sets and the defensive sets (like sagging man-for-man) he taught us. I used them when I was coaching youth "Y", and they worked.*

**Brian Sjodin '68** learned a lesson on varsity: *Mr. Musburger will always be Mr. Musburger to me. It was a real honor to have him as my coach. It was like one day I was shooting underhand and the next day, I was shooting 30-foot jump shots. That's how quick it went. I remember one practice Neil Wikstrom and I were in line shooting layups and Neil said something to me that coach overheard. He came over to us and told both of us to go down to the locker room and not come back until we were ready to play. So we went down to the locker room, looked at each other, and ran right back up. Practice was serious but fun. If we lost a game, it wasn't because we weren't prepared. We always knew what we were supposed to do. Those were the best of times.*

**Coach Musburger, Captain Neil Wikstrom, Coach Heck**
(1965 Karlstad Bluebook)

Team manager **Mark Erickson '67** and Coach Musburger shared an attention to detail and orderliness: *Mr. Musburger liked things clean, neat and orderly like me, so I swept the floor once a week and kept the shelves dusted and orderly and the uniforms well hung so they could air out before the next game. There were six balls set aside to be used only on game days. It was my job to scour the outside of the balls to remove any streaks and when they dried off, I would apply a special polish and buff them with an old towel. I really liked doing this because I knew this was important to Mr. Musburger, and I wanted to please him. Coach would often give me the keys to the school owned Ford station wagon, so I could drive uptown to get the previous week's towels that had been laundered at Naverud's Cleaning and Laundry Service at Thief River Falls or to pick up a case of Dial soap, both delivered to my parent's Hartz grocery store. Looking back, I felt Mr. Musburger's trust and* *affirmation. During practices, I needed to be available for equipment or medical needs and enjoyed listening to Coach's verbal interaction with the team. Hard work was expected but there was also joking and laughter.*

*Before every home game, I would go to the Home Economics room, arrange chairs into a circle for the team, and have Coca Cola chilling in the fridge. At the end of the game, I gathered uniforms and towels for the laundry bags. I was even given the job of calling in final scores and game details to a list of newspapers, radio stations and television stations. Initially, I felt very insecure, but I grew to like this. By the time all my tasks were completed, it was just me and the night custodian, either Henry Peterson or Bob Vik, left in the building. It was a quiet walk from the school to Hanson's Café where I gathered with other kids for French fries and a chocolate malt.*

*Away games were always stressful. I was responsible to keep the medicine chest well stocked and loaded on the bus along with two canvas bags each designed to carry three balls. Those balls, of course, were cleaned and shined. I also had to pack the uniforms in really large metal trunks and load them onto the bus. I remember the time I forgot to load the medicine chest on the bus and realized my mistake on the way to Strandquist. I had to build up the courage to tell Coach what happened but did not get chewed out. We phoned Leon Oistad and he delivered it to us.*

*On many game days, I sat at the scoreboard table and kept track of our team's fouls and points. It was important to be accurate and I remember feeling the weight of this. This also gave me the opportunity to meet the other team's scorekeeper, and we would compare our class rings and other things of great importance to us. When I didn't sit at the scoreboard table, I sat next to Mr. Musburger at every game. I clearly remember how his body moved with every shot, rebound, or block, with some sort of audible word or sound to accompany it. He was always fully engaged in what was happening on the court. I clearly remember a district game in Roseau when the excitement was over the top, and I was chewing Yucatan gum. Coach asked me for a piece of my gum. We won the game and from then on, Coach chewed Yucatan gum for every game. Coach trusted me and this gave me encouragement.*

**B Team1964-1965: Season Record: 5 wins, 4 losses. Kneeling: Dave Berg, Mike Folland, John Nelson, Greg Johnson, Mark Holter, Coach Gray. Standing: Harlan Bengtson, Stuart Spilde, Jan Nordin, Lowell Sjodin, Chuck Johnson, Mike McNelly, Reed Skogerboe.** (1965 Karlstad Bluebook)

Duane Heck and Jim Musburger coached the football team from a winless season the year before to a conference record 2-7 with victories over Kennedy 6-0 and Newfolden 13-7. Led by captain Hollis Turnwall, the team roster included Brian Sjodin, Ernie Pietruszewski, David Henry, Tom Folland, Duane Fish, Mark McNelly, Danny Nordine, Neil Skogerboe, Curtis Farbo, Neil Wikstrom, Tim Olson, Billy Struck, Randy Krantz, Mike Folland, Roger Golby, Ken Sylskar, Curtis Anderson, John Lund, Chuck Johnson, John Nelson and managers Mark Erickson and Paul Bostrom.

**Tim Olson** played on the '64-65 football team: *Duane Heck and Jim Musburger installed discipline and football knowledge into the team. I know Musburger was the line coach and Heck was the backfield coach. But they made a great team, both in football and basketball. Our first few games that first year we were somewhat competitive but lost them all. Our defense was tough, with guys like Curtis Anderson, Danny Nordine and Hollis Turnwall leading us. But our offense was a work in progress. Still, we broke the losing streak and we were no longer total losers. We lost to Stephen 7-6 that year, and Greenbush 7-0, and*

55

*Lancaster 13-7, so we were a good defensive team.*

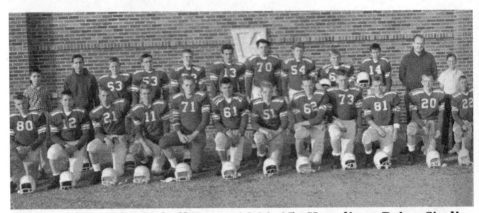

**Karlstad Varsity Football Team 1964-65: Kneeling: Brian Sjodin, Ernie Pietruszewski, Hollis Turnwall, David Henry, Tom Folland, Duane Fish, Mark McNelly, Neil Skogerboe, Curtis Farbo, Neil Wikstrom, Tim Olson, Bill Struck. Standing: Mark Erickson, manager, Coach Heck, Randy Krantz, John Folland, Roger Golby, Ken Sylskar, Curtis Anderson, John Lund, Chuck Johnson, John Nelson, Coach Musburger, Paul Bostrom, manager.**
(1965 Karlstad Bluebook)

Team manager **Paul Bostrom '67** recalls: *I played 7th and 8th grade and a little B squad for Mr. Musburger. But I was always a great fan of Coach Musburger and his teams. There isn't anybody that coaches like him anymore.*

Football Captain Hollis
Turnwall with Coaches Heck
and Musburger.

Varsity cheerleaders:
Genevieve Torkelson,
Virginia Olson, Karen
Stavenau, Peggy Spilde and
Connie Stamnes

1965 Golf Team
Left to right:  John Oistad, Craig Spilde, Greg Oistad, Jack Oistad,
Brian Sjodin, Steve Spilde, Stuart Spilde, Coach Musburger
(1965 Karlstad Bluebook)

## 10. KARLSTAD RABBITS 1965-66

*Yes, we are proud of our district champions, not only for their basketball prowess, but because of the type of boys they are, high-spirited, full of the old nick, but gentlemen all the way.* –Dane Nordine, *Karlstad Advocate*

Varsity players on the legendary 1966 district championship season were seniors and co-captains Dave Henry and Neil Wikstrom, Neil Skogerboe, Troy Dagen, Tom Folland and Glenn Pederson; juniors Tim Olson and Ernie Pietruszewski; sophomores Brian Sjodin and Jack Oistad and freshman Lowell Sjodin. Neil Wikstrom and Brian Sjodin won all conference honors, Troy Dagen was the free-throw champ and Tim Olson was named captain for the next year.

**Karlstad Varsity Basketball Team 1965-66: Kneeling: M. Erickson, manager, D. Henry, N. Wikstrom, D. Sylskar, manager. Standing: Coach Musburger, J. Oistad, B. Sjodin, E. Pietruszewski, G. Oistad, G. Pedersen, T. Folland, N. Skogerboe, T. Dagen, T. Olson, L. Sjodin, Coach Heck.** (1966 Karlstad Bluebook)

Coach Musburger opened the 1965-66 basketball season with a different approach. **Tim Olson** recalls the first day of practice: *When I was a junior, our first basketball practice of the season was ready to start. But instead of throwing out a bunch of basketballs and starting shooting or layups, he had us all go sit down on the bleachers. He brought out a chalkboard and proceeded to write down the names of* *the towns in our conference in order of where we ranked in the conference, picked by the coaches of the conference. We had been picked 6th, behind Argyle, Stephen, Kennedy, Hallock, and Lancaster. I was somewhat shocked and annoyed. We, as a team, had everyone back from the previous year. EVERYONE. How could those coaches disrespect us like that? I personally felt that we were going to be pretty good, because we had everyone returning and other teams had lost some good players. Well, it played out the way I thought, not the way the coach's thought.*

*The funny thing was, coach Musburger never sat us down in the bleachers before the season when I was a sophomore nor when I was a senior. Just that one year. I think that was his way of letting all of us know that we needed to earn that respect, and giving us a goal for the season. Whether that was the plan or not, we won the district that season.*

Team members treasured practice throughout the year on Saturday mornings. Tim recalls one Saturday morning when uninvited guests arrived: *One time on a Saturday, there was open Jim. Now you might think it is supposed to be open gym. Who knows, he just said there would be open Jim tomorrow, and that is what we heard. I was a sophomore, and there were three seniors, not players, that came in the school that morning, too. And how I got to town on a Saturday, being we still lived in the country, is a mystery that shall remain. But I was there, and the boss, the guy who would sacrifice his Saturday morning so that young basketball fanatics could go and shoot in the gym, which was always more fun when there were a few guys there. It was never much fun to shoot alone. Anyway, those three non-basketball players were not supposed to be in the school when school was not in session. So the boss told them that they were not allowed in the school and to leave. To close the story quickly, the boss went into the entrance room with a basketball, where the trophies were kept on display. Then we heard, "I TOLD YOU TO GET THE HELL OUT OF HERE," followed by a very loud breaking of glass. The boss had thrown the basketball at those people who did not want to leave very quickly, missed, and broke a glass window by the entrance door. Needless to say, all the shooters were VERY mild mannered for the rest of the shoot around.*

**Neil Skogerboe** offers his varsity perspective: *Mr. Musburger moved up to A team coach when I was a Junior. He frequently said we should play for the fun of it, and would add, "It's no fun to lose." Practices were serious but fun. We all knew he was good hearted, but he also had a temper that no one wanted to trigger. He treated everybody the same. He probably liked some of us more than others, but that did not exempt us from his occasional wrath.*

*In the spring of my junior year, after the basketball season, he gave me a key to the school and the equipment room. He told me to keep everybody in the gym or locker room. We played many hours of basketball - late at night, early morning, whenever we could get together. This lasted through the summer. I don't think he asked anybody about this, but just did it.*

*We were a fairly small team. I was 6 feet even and played center. Most of my opponents were taller, but I got a large majority of the jump ball tips. I would set up with my left shoulder toward the center and rotate when I jumped to tip the ball with my right hand, brushing the opponent's body downward with my left hand. Most didn't ever notice. I got called for a foul once after which Mr. Musburger said I needed to be more subtle. Many of the games we played would be fairly close after three quarters. Then we would turn up the tempo and run away with the game. We were in better condition than most of the teams we played. One game I was not being very productive and at halftime, he turned to me and said, "You have a hundred moves - use some!" I had a good second half - 20 points. He was a great motivator.*

*We played in the District Championship game and won - only four turnovers, and we were off to the Region 8 tournament. Coach got a call from the Minneapolis Tribune and was asked to describe our team. He said, "We're small - but we're slow." (We were not slow). In the program for the regional tournament, he listed each of our heights at least two inches shorter than we were. I was listed at 5'10" and Brian Sjodin was listed at 5'4". We did not play our usual basketball that night, more than 20 turnovers contributed to a loss. We all felt we let Coach Musburger down. But overall it was a good season and it was a joy to play for him.*

**Coach Musburger** commented that following the loss in the regional tournament, the referee told him that the Rabbits made more turnovers that game (22) than he had seen the team make all year. Coach also relayed that Neil Skogerboe recently told him that the team got into a fight with Stephen players after a conference game, and that he (Neil) got a black eye.

**Tim Olson** vividly remembers the referees: *The bozos we had at that game wouldn't have known a charge if it bit them in the ass. We were getting killed on that, because a lot of our game was 'move your feet', thereby getting in position to draw a charge. Neil Skogerboe got flattened at least three times and nothing was called. And going over the back on rebounds didn't draw a whistle, either.*

**Coach Musburger** also remembered Neil Skogerboe missing the bus: *I was very prompt about leaving on time for games. I would say to the bus driver, "Harry, let's go!" Once, Neil was late for a bus trip to Kennedy and we had to leave him behind. Pretty soon, I would see Dr. Skogerboe roaring behind us in their station wagon with Neil in tow. This happened more than once.*

**Tim Olson** recounts coming into the '65-'66 season: *I thought we were pretty confident, but untested. Before Christmas vacation, we had four ball games. The only one I remember was the one against Lake Bronson. Both times we played them that year, it was a gang fight. We won both games, but what a struggle. They even won the district four years earlier, and finished second three years earlier. They raised them mean back then. After Christmas vacation, we played East Grand Forks Sacred Heart. They had a good team, led by 6'5" Jim Hoffert and two other good players, a Marek and a Demers. They made it to the state in a Catholic league that year. Anyway, we were both undefeated before that game and played at Karlstad. The gym was full because Sacred Heart had been hyped up in the Grand Forks Herald prior to the game, and rightfully so. We really worked hard that game and it was tight the whole way, but that Hoffert was just too much. And his best shot was probably a 25- footer. A smooth left-hander. We lost 60-54. But coach was proud of our effort, and the outcome could have gone either way.*
 *Next game was Stephen at Stephen when Stephen had that small gym that doubled as a stage. And they were FAMOUS for their box press.*

They would put it on and even good teams would wither and melt under that pressure. So for two days of practice before that game, Musburger put on his box press against the starters. He had every reserve, and a couple of extra B team players, on the floor while we had to move the ball up the court. All practice long, that is what we did, against eight or nine defenders. After those practices, we were so good at breaking that press that we couldn't wait to get to Stephen. And guess what. Stephen never once put that press on the entire game. Threw us all out of whack. We lost 60-54.

Next game was at Middle River. Knew nothing about them, except that two years earlier they had won the district, and still had some players back from that team. And Coach said that he had heard that they "had a barnburner" that year. Well, Neil Skogerboe was sick, so he missed that game. Which meant that we were shorthanded a bit. And their gym was a little smaller than ours. They came out in a zone defense, and it seemed like we were playing in a forest, with trees all over the place. They played that zone really well, we did not, and lost that game 64-53. So here we are, seven games into our season and sitting on a 4-3 record. Well, we finished off the regular season and district tournament winning 16 of our next 17 games, going to Grand Forks with a 20-4 record.

And thinking back, was it just a coincidence that we played Middle River early in the season? I bet coach planned that out. Just like he had us playing both Baudette (district champ in '67) and Bemidji in '67. Never gave it a thought before, but it was coach making plans for the future, getting his team ready for tournaments, always planning for the future. Coach sure had his angles. We were too young to know it at the time.

Stephen Coach **Jim Schindele** reflects on his rivalry with Coach Musburger: *I had great respect for Jim both on and off the basketball court. We were very competitive coaches and enjoyed every minute of the game – win or lose. One thing that got Jim's attention and the fans too, was when someone let five rabbits out on the court before the game. I said I wasn't behind it, but that some Stephen fans were the culprits. It was quite a commotion! I retired from coaching in 1966 and took on the principal's position at Stephen. It was a difficult decision because I loved coaching.*

When the 1965-66 Rabbits tied Lancaster for the Northern Lights conference title (14-2), Dane Nordine, publisher of the *Karlstad Advocate*, proudly wrote: *The Karlstad Rabbits, smarting from their defeat at the hands of the Argyle Eagles, turned on the Lancaster Cardinals with a vengeance Friday night and whipped their conference co-champions 60-36. The Rabbits put together what probably was their best full-game performance of the season. David Henry, regular Rabbit forward, was in the ball game at the opening whistle in spite of an injury, but after one play, he was replaced by Ernie Pietruszewski who saw action at that spot most of the remainder of the way – and what a ball game he played, but then, who didn't? Brian Sjodin, the Karlstad pepper pot, picked up three early fouls and was replaced by Troy Dagen, who held his ground through the second quarter as the Rabbits were making their move. Tim Olson came up with one of his better scoring nights in recent weeks and played beautifully on the boards. Neil Skogerboe led the scoring attack for Karlstad garnering 19 points to drive for his baskets. Neil Wikstrom, that little senior guard who is going to be hard to replace next year, probably popped in the two key buckets of the ball game.*

**1966 Captains David Henry and Neil Wikstrom**
(1966 Karlstad Bluebook)

**David Spilde '79** shares a memory: *When I was five years old, David Henry was my idol. He wore a knee brace for basketball and so I would wrap a towel around my knee and shoot baskets endlessly into a garbage can on the farm.*

The Rabbits continued their run in the sub-district tournament by rolling over Kennedy 81-59 and Stephen 80-48 to reach the championship game with Lancaster. Brian Sjodin led the way with 25 points to trounce the Cardinals 68-46. Lancaster's big man, Perry Pearson, scored 30 points for the Cardinals. But the Rabbits quest for success marched on as they defeated Roseau 84-54, edged archrival Stephen 54-50 and finally, Middle River 66-55 to win the District 32 title and advance to the Region 8 tournament in Grand Forks.

**Tim Olson** recalls: *The best part of the year was beating Stephen three times that year, including the district semifinal game, and then beating Middle River in the finals. We were so determined in the finals, and played one of our best, if not the best game of the year. Everyone was "on," and every point was defended. We never gave an inch the entire game. Middle River was tough. Their best player, Eldon Sparby, got me for 25 points the first game of the season. I scored 11. So I personally wanted to get him back the second time. I stuck to him like a wood tick on a dog, held him to 17, and scored 16. He really was one tough mother. He went on to become a teacher and coach for Middle River, and even coached against Musburger.* Dave Henry and Tim Olson each had 16 points while Eldon Sparby and Steve Holmes scored 17 and 14 points respectively for the Skippers.

Middle River's **Eldon Sparby** offers his perspective: *As a player I can remember hoping we would play Karlstad early in the season. The comment that "Rome wasn't built in a day," is very fitting for Coach Musburger! The later in the season, the tougher it was to beat him. We always knew it didn't matter how much talent he had on the court, the Rabbits were going to be tough to score against and never an easy win. I didn't realize how great a job he would do at taking out the other team's best player. My senior year we had played the Rabbits early in the season and won by about 15 points. I remember thinking I hoped someone would knock them out of the tournament so we wouldn't have to meet them again.*

*However, we did end up facing off with the Rabbits again and this time without our starting center. We lost him to a severely sprained ankle in the semi-finals and he was not able to play. He had caused the Rabbits some headaches in the first meeting and it was enough to give us a win first time around. Without him I was double covered and had a terrible night to even get a look at the basket. I will never forget that night and my frustration with my teammates. They all went into the game overconfident that we were going to win! Coach Musburger took me out of the offense and allowed our confident players all the shots they wanted. They did not hit and we were out rebounded. Rabbits beat the Skippers with what I felt was not as good a team, but an outstanding defense that we could not handle. I learned great defense is not fun to play against.*

*When I started coaching as a rookie, I was competing against Coaches Musburger, Deere, Keller, Ron Ueland and Gary Schuler. Talk about jumping into the fire and not knowing a damn thing about coaching. I quickly learned that if you want to beat the best, you better figure out what they are doing to you and how are you going to compete. Coach Musburger was my first model who I tried to emulate. First because of my experience as an athlete and secondly, I appreciated his game coaching behaviors and the way he always treated his athletes with respect. You always knew what was coming when you played the Rabbits: sagging man to man and always taking away your best player option. The comment made about teams thinking they were playing against a zone because his kids sagged so much, is absolutely true. I remember scouting his team and seeing other teams trying to beat him with a zone offense. I believe he won way more games than his talent should have won. Coach Musburger's teams always outworked their opponents and this proved a formula for success for him and I tried to do the same with my teams.*

*He was a very professional and respectful coach to all his peers. I appreciated that as a rookie and tried to model that trait all my years of coaching. His teams never beat themselves, his teams seldom turned the ball over, and even though most times outsized, I doubt he was out rebounded very often. Coach Musburger was a great coach and anyone who learned the game from him was blessed.*

After winning the District 32 championship, **Dane Nordine** once again portrayed the immense community pride and spirit in the 1966 team: *Basketball has taken over our village and our area this week. Whether it's a ladies coffee party or a group of men standing on the corner, or a student seemingly looking over his books, the word "basketball" is forever creeping into the conversation or thoughts. Chances are good were there to be a local election this day, Mayor Oistad's job would be in a precarious position, for it wouldn't surprise us one bit if the name "Jim Musburger" would find its way on many a ballot in the write-in spot. We're certainly proud of our boys and their coach. The lads have played their hearts out time and time again this season and their coach has provided them with the temperament and the strategy needed to make them giant killers. Usually the goal from this district is to make it to the region, but with this group of surprising ball players, well, anything can happen. They are too small, but they've been too small all year and we're certain they will be in Grand Forks to play ball. The support this basketball team has had from the student body and the local populace has also been fabulous; and while the players probably do not hear each individual as he shouts his words of encouragement, they do hear the din and know they have the backing – this is important. There have been people attending games this year who have not ventured to the gym for some time. Students from the various colleges were home in force for that final contest at Roseau and other local fans came from many points in the state to urge the youngsters on.*

No one can say that **Dane** lacked a sense of humor. He ends his column with vivid descriptions of loyal supporters: *Local fans have indeed been ardent this year, but some of the more modest people were a bit afraid Virgil Hams was to do a complete strip before one of the district games was over. He looked so nice when he came dressed in suit and tie, but each time one looked over at him, he had another piece of clothing removed and he was nearly down to his T-shirt and shorts before the final whistle blew. Then there was another vociferous fellow from here (John Oistad) who had to go diving for his upper plate when he spewed that out in the middle of one of his cheers.*

*Coach Jim Musburger's father drove over from Bemidji just to see the final game at Roseau – you have never seen anyone more proud. And how about those Halma fans? There are three or four families over there that we'd dare say didn't miss a game all season. Yes, we are proud of our district champions, not only for their basketball prowess, but because of the type of boys they are, high-spirited, full of the old nick, but gentlemen all the way.*

*We're probably talking out of school, but the story also goes that the Middle River coach, Jerry Snyder – who incidentally, has always had a lot of respect from this corner – congratulated Musburger following the game. When Musburger mentioned that it was too bad that Kirk Holmes had to sit on the bench with a bad leg in this game, Mr. Snyder's reply is said to have gone something like this: "You made no alibis when we defeated you earlier in the season when you had to leave your center, Skogerboe, at home with the flu; we'll make no alibis now. We're behind you." Sports are a wonderful thing, and there are some wonderful people in them. (14 March 1966, Karlstad Advocate)*

**Jerry Snyder** recounts 1966: *I coached in Middle River from 1961-66. The first time I saw Musburger's team play, I was on a scouting trip and my impression was, 'this is a well-coached team.' Middle River didn't have any games with Karlstad until my last year at Middle River. In a non-conference regular season game at Middle River, we prevailed. If I remember correctly, that year (1966), a blizzard caused postponements of the West Sub-District Tournament. The West didn't complete their tournament until Monday of District week, which meant that the West team that reached the finals of the District 32 Tournament would be playing four games that week – a very demanding task.*

*Karlstad and Middle River both won their quarterfinal and semi-final games and met for the District 32 championship. All I remember is that Karlstad won, and that I admired and respected Musburger's coaching and his players for their accomplishment.*

Although the mighty Rabbits lost to Thief River Falls 49-41 and to Bemidji 77-56 in the regional tournament, they won the hearts of their fans forever with their season record 20-6.

Following the regional tournament, **Dane Nordine** wrote: *Our hats are off to that group of basketball players who represented District 32 in the regional tournament at Grand Forks over the weekend. The Karlstad Rabbits didn't do any winning over there, but when you consider this is only the fourth group of local lads who have ever made it that far in basketball, and when you consider their size, you just have to admit that they have done mighty well. This group of boys, who under Coach Jim Musburger and his assistant Duane Heck, have kept themselves in superlative condition, have probably given local fans their most thrilling year ever. We've had other fine ball clubs here, but we doubt we've ever had a winning group that succeeded against such great odds as this plucky group.* (21 March 1966, *Karlstad Advocate*)

**B Team 1965-66: Row 1: K. Berg, J. Oistad, J. Nelson, J. Nordin, P. Bostrom. Row 2: Coach Musburger, L. Sjodin, D. Berg, T. Nordin, C. Spilde, G. Oistad, Coach Heck.** (1966 Karlstad Bluebook)

TUESDAY, MARCH 8 –

7:00 p.m. – Roseau vs Karlstad
8:30 p.m. – Badger vs Stephen

WEDNESDAY, MARCH 9 –

7:00 p.m. – Middle River vs Kennedy
8:30 p.m. – Baudette vs Lancaster

FRIDAY, MARCH 11 –

7:00 p.m. —Winners of Tuesday night games
8:30 p.m.—Winners of Wednesday night games

SATURDAY, March 12 –

7:00 p.m.—Consolation game
8:30 p.m. Championship game

The winner of the district 32 championship will advance to the region 8 tournament on Friday and Saturday, March 18 and 19, at the field house at the University of North Dakota at Grand Forks.

# 1966
# DISTRICT 32

Minnesota State High School League

# BASKETBALL TOURNAMENT

ROSEAU HIGH SCHOOL AUDITORIUM

# MARCH 8, 9, 11, 12

REFEREES: Bill Galloway and G. V. Shipley of Park River, N. Dak.

Official Tournament Band – Roseau

Plus guest bands from competing schools

Tournament Manager: R. J. Halvorson

**1966 District 32 Tournament program**

Led by seniors Duane Fish, Tom Folland, Curtis Farbo, Troy Dagen, David Henry, Neil Skogerboe (captain), and Neil Wikstrom, the 1966 varsity football team improved their season record to 3-4-1.  The Rabbits defeated Argyle, Stephen and Newfolden, lost to Hallock, Baudette, Warroad and Stephen, and tied Lancaster.  Juniors Randy Krantz, Mark Vagle, Roger Golby, Ron Anderson, Ernie Pietruszewski, Tim Olson, Gary Hultgren, Donnie Wollin, and sophomores Ken Sylskar, Brian Sjodin, Chuck Johnson, Greg Johnson, Greg Oistad, Mike Folland and John Nelson filled out the roster.

 Neil Wikstrom and David Henry were named All-Conference.

**Karlstad Varsity Football Team 1965-66: Kneeling: B. Sjodin, E. Pietruszewski, H. Turnwall, D. Henry, T. Folland, D. Fish, M. McNelly, N. Skogerboe, C. Farbo, N. Wikstrom, T. Olson, B. Struck. Standing: M. Erickson, manager, Coach Heck, R. Krantz, J. Folland, R. Golby, K. Sylskar, C. Anderson, J. Lund, C. Johnson, J. Nelson, Coach Musburger, P. Bostrom, manager.** (1966 Bluebook)

Varsity players were not without a sense of humor either. Tim Olson recalls Neil Skogerboe's favorite saying: *"If at first you don't succeed, keep on sucking 'til you do suckceed."* And David Henry threw in a humorous football memory: *Most vivid memory of a specific thing was coach having us hold leg lifts 6 inches off the ground and then walking across our stomachs during football practice. Still makes me smile and maybe cringe just a little .*

**1966 Seniors: Front row: Duane Fish, Tom Folland, Curtis Farbo. Back row: Troy Dagen, David Henry, Neil Skogerboe, Neil Wikstrom** (1966 Bluebook)

**1965-66 Captain
Neil Skogerboe**

**1966-1967
Captain
Ernie
Pietruszewski**

**Varsity Cheerleaders 1965-66:  Maryel  Anderson, Sheila
Nordine, Virginia Olson, Peggy Spilde and Genevieve Torkelson.**
(1966 Bluebook)

Cheerleader **Sheila Nordine'68** shares  an experience off the court:  *I
certainly have a story that I remember like it was yesterday because I
was so embarrassed when it happened.  It was "shot" day and I was
terrified of needles.  I was in Mr. Musburger's class when the time
arrived for our shots.  He escorted the class down to the gym where we
all received our shots.  When it was my turn, I fainted dead away.  Poor
Mr. Musburger had to carry me up two steep staircases all the way back*

71

*to the classroom. When I woke up, he teased me. That helped a bit, but I felt so bad that he had to carry me up those awful stairs!*

**B Team Cheerleaders: Celeste Dagen, Garnette Pederson, Leta Stavenau, Janakaye Dagen**

**C Team cheerleaders: Jill Musburger, Paulette Oien, Colleen Koland, Carole Anderson, Jolane Olson** (1966 Bluebook)

## 11. KARLSTAD RABBITS 1966-67

*I always say that you start with a good coach and players that get along together and have fun.* – Ernie Pietruszewski '67

The 1966-67 basketball team had a tough act to follow but they valiantly matched the record of the 1965-66 team. Varsity team members included Tim Nordin, Craig Spilde, Jerry Kuznia, Jan Nordin, John Nelson, Ernie Pietruszewski, Brian Sjodin, Tim Olson, Greg Oistad, Jack Oistad, Stuart Spilde, Lowell Sjodin, manager Mark Erickson, and coaches Jim Musburger and Duane Heck. Tim Olson, Brian and Ernie were all-conference selections. Cheerleaders were Celeste Dagen, Peggy Seng, Peggy Spilde, Sheila Nordine and Maryel Anderson (captain). A season record of 14 wins and 4 losses (Baudette, Stephen, Argyle and Bemidji) earned the team co-conference champion honors with Lancaster. The Rabbits won the sub-district by steamrolling over Humboldt 66-49 and Hallock 57-42 before defeating Stephen in a thrilling 52-51 game. But the Rabbits were denied a trip to the regional tournament when they fell to Argyle 38-33 in the semi-finals and placed third in the district by trouncing Stephen 64-51.

Argyle's **Conrad Lubarski '69** remembers when Argyle edged Karlstad: *If my memory serves me right, Argyle was defeated by Baudette in the district championship in '67. We had a premier post player in Mark Newman. It was also fun playing on the same team with my brother, Richard, who was 2 years old than I.* Conrad's teammate **Mark Newman '67** commented: *Just ask Coach Musburger what team was the biggest thorn in their side! Argyle played Karlstad six times and we beat them five out of the six. That semifinal game against Karlstad was nerve wracking, white knuckles the whole game. We knew we had to play our best against Karlstad and couldn't make mistakes in order to win. They had a better perimeter game and we had a better inside game. Our 1-3-1 zone defense beat their sagging man to man – Brian and Ernie would try to steal the ball. I had 22 points that game. Baudette beat us for the district championship but they had a better team. And here's a bit of trivia for you: Most of the players in our sub-district were first cousins and they were excellent athletes.*

**Varsity Basketball Team 1966-67: Left to right: T. Nordin, C. Spilde, J. Kuznia, J. Nordin, J. Nelson, E. Pietruszewski, B. Sjodin, T. Olson, G. Oistad, J. Oistad, S. Spilde, L. Sjodin. Center: Coach Musburger and Coach Heck** (1967 Bluebook)

**Tim Olson** compares his senior year team to the 1966 team: *This isn't so much a story about James Musburger as it is about his coaching prowess. He was the one that would say 'MOVE YOUR FEET' when teaching us defense. In 1965-66 we had a pretty good team. I think it was the first district championship team to visit Karlstad for at about twelve years. But this is about next year. Six seniors had graduated from the team: Neil Wikstrom, Neil Skogerboe, Dave Henry, Troy Dagen, Tom Folland and Glenn Pederson. Brian and I had started that year and Ernie was 6th man. Our team got better late in the season when Lowell Sjodin, a freshman, joined the starting lineup. Most of the guys still had football legs when the season started, Brian, of course, being the exception. Brian could go all year, not pick up a golf club, and still swing it on Dec. 31. He was just one of those naturals.*

*Anyway, our first game of the year is against Baudette, up at Baudette, a long bus ride. They had lost in the district semifinals the year before to Middle River, and had most of their team back. We got killed. We did not play well, were not used to playing with each other, and it showed. We lost by 20, just not any worse than that. We also lost our last* regular season game that year at Bemidji, another long bus ride, by around 20. But we had an excuse that game. Brian, Greg, and I got sick on the bus ride down, we played, but I am quite sure we would have given them a better game if we had felt ok. We played a 16 game regular season, so our '66-67 team lost four regular season games. The '65-66 team lost 4 regular season games. The difference was the '67 team lost in the semifinals of the district in overtime to Argyle. Our other two losses during the regular season were to Stephen, on their bandbox court and to Argyle by one point on our home court. So not counting the region losses, the '66 team went 20-4, the '67 team went 19-5. Baudette did win the district in 67, we were hoping for a rematch, but didn't get one. Our loss to Argyle on our home court during the regular season was the one and only time a strategy by the head coach backfired. It is the end of the game, about five or so seconds left. We have a one-point lead AND the ball out of bounds at midcourt. In the huddle, Musburger tells us instead of passing the ball into the frontcourt and probably getting fouled right away, he tells Brian to run into the backcourt, pass the ball to him, and Brian being such a good dribbler, could just dribble away the last few seconds, ergo ballgame. It started out that way, but there was a rough spot on the floor where the boards were funky, and the ball bounced crazily, right into the hands of an Argyle defender. The guy went in for a layup at the buzzer and we lost. Part of the board had heaved up a bit, and the dribble hit at exactly that spot, and boinked away. So, if it hadn't been for that stupid board, we in '67 would have also finished 20-4. But he still took a team that was not as good as the one the year before, and almost got the same results. Of course, we know he was good because he got results like that too many times. The only part of that Argyle game I remember was the ending, and I still remember thinking what a great strategy that was. That call could have been made 100 times, and 99 times it would have worked except this one time.

**Brian Sjodin** echoes the same memory: *I remember the Argyle game at home. I was dribbling the ball and the ball hit the spot on the floor that was warped by the scorer's table from a leaky roof. I went one way and the ball another, and Argyle scored on a layup and won the game.*

Argyle's **Connie Lubarski** did not forget that game: *I do remember the game Brian Sjodin referred to, and it was unbelievable to me that he* *lost the ball on the dribble and we scored and won.  Brian was such an excellent basketball player and a superb athlete in all sports, as was his younger brother Lowell.*  Argyle's **Mark Newman** vividly recalls:  *That game was the biggest fluke of all time.  After Brian lost the ball, Glen Schmidt went in for a lay-up and we scored.  I was ready for the rebound but we were out of time.*

**Ernie Pietruszewski '67** played varsity three years from '64-67:  *We had some very good basketball teams at Karlstad High School in the 60's and 70's.  The teams in our conference during '64-67 were all very good teams.  We were usually smaller than the other teams, in fact, I think we only had three or four kids that were even 6'.  We might have had one player that made it to 6'1".  Wayne Ruud played for Middle River and he was really tall.  We had to play our best basketball against any of the teams to come out with a victory.  The teams I am talking about are Hallock, Kennedy, Humboldt, Argyle and Stephen on the west side, and Lancaster, Lake Bronson, Strandquist and my team, the Karlstad Rabbits.  I always say that you start with a good coach and players that get along together and have fun.  Our success started with practice and there was tough competition.  We worked hard especially if you were on the second unit playing against the starters.  I know this made us better.  I liked to try and get as many rebounds as I could.  Coach Musburger taught us way back when we were on the B and C teams to rebound by getting position.  I know I took that to heart and in games I could go up and pull down those rebounds.*

*I remember in practice dribbling with glasses so you couldn't see the ball, and figure eight drills often with a heavier medicine ball that you couldn't dribble.  You learned to pass and break down the floor without taking a dribble.  We had free throw contests usually once a week where you shot 25 free throws.  If you made the most free throws, Coach Musburger would buy you a hamburger basket or malt.  He would watch, and if you were in the lead, he would come over and try to make you miss by saying, "You can't make the next one."  Or if someone had a girlfriend, he would be sure to mention her name.  I remember that getting a burger basket or malt was great, so we would practice free throws every day.  When I was a sophomore and junior, I was usually the first sub into the game.  Coach Musburger would always have an empty chair right beside him for me.  He would rest his arm on my shoulder and tell me if someone did something wrong, and what they should have done. I always admired sitting next to coach. I called it learning on the job.*

*We would have tough games with all the teams in our conference especially when we were younger. As we got older, the smaller schools would have a tougher time. One thing is for sure, the opposing teams would always play their best. We had some tough losses, like the 1966 Region tournament playing Thief River Falls Prowlers when I was a junior. They had a good team with taller players. The first quarter we jumped out to a 19-6 lead and they called timeout. We ran off the court to get with Coach Musburger. The scoreboard at the UND Fieldhouse was up above you in the center. We were all unaware of our lead. Musburger talked about keeping the pressure on them, and then someone said something about holding the lead. The players looked up at the score and we couldn't believe that we had that big lead. After that, everything seemed to go wrong. We couldn't catch the ball and the turnovers killed us. We lost.*

*As a senior, we lost a lot of players from the year before, so we played with different starters. We had tough games with everyone again. Argyle, Stephen and Lancaster were very tough. In a game with Argyle in Karlstad, the game went into overtime, we had the lead and the ball with a few seconds left. The ball got away from us and they picked it up and scored. That was a tough loss on our floor.*

*Those three seasons of basketball were over 50 years ago and a person still replays those games in your head. I remember all the fans at our games, even away games, and the gyms were packed with people screaming. Doris Johnson from Halma never missed a game. Our great cheerleaders always led the way to get our fans going. I know that almost everyone in town would come to our games, just like one big happy family. My senior season was a lot of fun, going 8-0 in football, 19-5 in basketball and 14-0 winning the sub-district. We ended up losing to Baudette in the district, but indeed a fine year.*

**West Sub-District champs, Hallock: Left to right: Coach Musburger, Kent Hanson, Lowell Sjodin, Greg Oistad, Brian Sjodin, Jerry Kuznia, Tim Olson, Stuart Spilde, Tim Nordin, Jan Nordin, Ernie Pietruszewski, Craig Spilde, Jack Oistad.**
(2 March 1967 *Karlstad Advocate*)

**Lowell Sjodin '70** remembers Ernie during practice*: I remember when Neil Skogerboe played center. Coach would have Ernie Pietruszewski jump center because Ernie had the best vertical jump on the team. Ernie could stand under the rim and jump and grab the rim. Looked kind of funny to have the shortest guy on the team jump the tallest guy on the opposing team. Also, Coach allowed the alumni to practice against the current varsity squad. It was fun to have someone different to practice against.*

**Coach Musburger** said Ernie could out-rebound almost anyone, even a much taller Perry Pearson at Lancaster.

## 1967 Sub-District All Conference Players
(2 March 1967, *Karlstad Advocate*)

**Tim Olson** recounts a funny incident at the end of basketball season: *My senior year, the season is over. Musburger, as he was sometimes called, (never Jim or James) only among players, and never to his face. HE COMMANDED RESPECT. Anyway, after the season is over, he decides the seniors will play next year's team. So there is Ernie, Tim Nordin, Horse Gorsuch, Paul Bostrom, Ron Anderson and me, and we are anxious to play. Warm-ups, HIS team has eight basketballs to warm up, and we get one, and that one has no air in it. That was it. Was I ever pissed. And the game started with the score 30-0. Karl Carlson and Gary Cook were refs and did fine as officials. The game started and I wanted to kill the other team and especially their coach! I mean the other team had Brian and Lowell Sjodin, Greg and Jack Oistad, Craig Spilde, Jan Nordin and other younger players, too. After a few minutes (and a lot of bitching from me) the scoreboard was changed to the correct score. I was so upset with coach's actions that I played one of my best games ever. The final score ended in a tie – a good game for everybody. Maybe the coach should have made me angry before every game. Seemed to work that time. Never found out if he planned it that way, or he did it because we were no longer on "his team." I think he did what he did so we would remember it. If it had just been a get together* *with no drama, we would not remember it. It was a classic move by Coach Musburger. One of his favorite sayings was "you can't make a silk purse out of a sow's ear." I think I was a senior before I finally figured out we were sow's ears.*

**C Team 1967: Row 1: Richie Pietruszewski, Jon Nordine, Kent Hanson, Rick Falk, Ricky Simmons, Glen Spilde. Row 2: Coach Leon Oistad, Orlin Anderson, John Oistad, Jim Musburger, Jonathon Spilde, Devin Dagen, Lamar Gunnarson, Craig Bolin, manager. Row 3: Tom Stallock, John Erickson, Lyle Jacobson, Richie Simmons, Ron Bengtson.** (1967 Bluebook)

This talented '67 class, coached by Duane Heck and Jim Musburger, also went undefeated in football with a record 8 – 0 to win the Little Seven Conference championship. The Rabbits ended their perfect season by toppling Drayton 41-20 and outscored the other conference teams by 259 points to 73. Captains Randy Krantz and Tim Olson led the varsity team: Mike Folland, John Nelson, Ernie Pietruszewski, Mark Vagle, Jan Nordin, Steve Andersen, Robert Clark, Danny Sylskar, Kent Hanson, Donnie Anderson, Greg Johnson, Greg Oistad, Ron Anderson, Donnie Wollin, Ken Sylskar, Brian Sjodin, Chuck Johnson, Lowell Sjodin, Roger Golby, Jerry Kuznia, Stuart Spilde, Doug Larson and manager Mark Erickson. All-conference players were Brian Sjodin, Tim Olson, Ernie Pietruszewski, Mark Vagle and Don Wollin.

**Co-captain Randy Krantz** describes his football journey: *I remember when we were in 7th grade, and Brian Sjodin and I went out for football.*

*We had to practice with the Varsity squad, the big guys! We held the tackling dummies as the Varsity hit them. We were so much smaller than they were. It was a tough couple of years but Coach Musburger encouraged us to "hang in there." Actually, we got our ASSES kicked for the first couple of years, but it paid off a few years later. We both got tougher and meaner. When I was a junior, Karlstad hadn't won a game in many years, but our team won 3 games. The next year, our senior year, our record was 8 wins, 0 losses! I was the Defensive Captain of that team, and I know Coach Musburger had a lot to do with my being chosen for that. He was an excellent coach and my favorite teacher.*

**Varsity Football Team 1966-67** (1967 Bluebook)

Coach **Duane Heck** reminisces: *This undefeated '67 team stands out in my memory. Quarterback Tim Olson, running backs Brian Sjodin and Ernie Pietruszewski, and the whole team were really good. We often had undersized kids but they always performed far above their ability. When I left Karlstad in '68 for another job, I learned to appreciate Jim's line coaching skills as no one could match him. I only coached three more years after leaving Karlstad and I really enjoyed the school and kids there.*

**Coach Musburger** tells of a humorous incident after football practice: *Head coach Duane Heck was a great football coach and stern disciplinarian. I learned a lot from him. One day at the end of practice, Heck told the kids to pick up the dummies and take them back to the gym. One of the players, Chuck Johnson from Halma, picked up Heck. Everyone laughed, even Heck.*

**Karl Carlson**, music teacher at KHS, wrote: *Just imagine a coach and music teacher being great friends! I recall when Jim had a study hall.*

*Mr. Heck was the math teacher.  When the kids need help in math, Jim loved telling them to go to Heck.*

And to top off an amazing year, they also won the baseball sub-district championship with a perfect record 14-0 led by captain Tim Nordin and coach Leon Oistad.

Letterman's Club 1967:  Seated:  Mr. Heck, T. Olson, E. Pietruszewski, T. Nordin, Mr. Musburger.  Row 1:  S. Andersen D. Larson, S. Spilde, D. Sylskar, J. Nordin, R. Koland, M. Folland, M. Erickson.  Row 2:  R. Golby, K. Hanson, J. Kuznia, C. Spilde, J. Stallock, J. Nelson, G. Johnson, R. Clark.  Row 3:  R. Krantz, B. Sjodin, J. Oistad, G. Oistad, L. Sjodin, M. Vagle, R. Anderson, K. Sylskar, D. Wollin.

**Peggy Seng '69**
(1967 Bluebook)

## 12. KARLSTAD RABBITS 1967-68

*I was guarding a kid by the name of Dean Carlson. Coach told me, "Deny him the ball. Wherever he goes you go. If he goes to the locker room, you go with him."* – Greg Oistad '68 on the sub-district championship game with Hallock.

The 1968 basketball team surprised everyone, including Coach Musburger, by defeating Kennedy 45-43, Argyle 54-51, and Hallock 56-5, in white-knuckle games to win the sub-district title. Although they previously lost their games to all three teams in regular season play, this scrappy Rabbit team delivered the championship trophy. Seniors John Nelson, Greg Oistad, Brian Sjodin (captain), Jack Oistad and Craig Spilde led the varsity team. Other team members included Jerry Pietruszewski, Jerry Kuznia, Kent Hanson, Stuart Spilde, Harlan Bengtson, Chris Johnson and Lowell Sjodin. Brian was selected for all-conference honors.

**Varsity Basketball 1968: Left to right: J. Pietruszewski, J. Kuznia, K. Hanson, S. Spilde, H. Bengtson, J. Nelson, B. Sjodin, J. Oistad, C. Johnson, C. Spilde, G. Oistad, L. Sjodin.** (1968 Bluebook)

**Greg Oistad '68** describes the surprise victory: *We were playing Hallock for the sub-district championship in 1968. Hallock had us by 2-3 inches at every position. Lowell Sjodin (Stretch) was guarding a kid by the name of Charlie Trolin. Trolin was about 4" taller than Lowell*

83

and had him by at least 50 lbs.  Coach told Lowell to lean on Trolin and make him work for everything he got.  Coach said we would let Trolin have 30 points and we would shut everybody else down.  I was guarding a kid by the name of Dean Carlson.  He told me, "Deny him the ball.  Wherever he goes you go.  If he goes to the locker room, you go with him."  At halftime we were down by 10 - 12 points.  Coach came into the locker room and said, "We got them right where we want them.  Trolin will be so tired by the end of the game he won't be able to lift his arms to shoot."  We ended up winning the game 56-51.

**Tim Olson** watched the game:  *And Trolin was more than a kid.  He was a senior, and Lowell was a sophomore.  Trolin would bounce from one side of the three-second lane to the other, back and forth.  They would pass the ball to him, he would be about four to five feet from the basket, turn and shoot.  And bank it in.  He had it down to a science.  Then at the end, Lowell reached across and stole the ball.  Karlstad scored to go ahead and held on.*

**1968 Sub-District champions:  Seniors John Nelson, Greg Oistad, Brian Sjodin, Jack Oistad, Craig Spilde**
(7 March 1968 *Karlstad Advocate*)

84

**Coach Musburger** commented: *We should never have won the sub-district. Our season record was 10-8, but the boys would not give up. Greg and Lowell stepped up and played their best games ever.*

**Coach Jim Musburger, Captain Brian Sjodin, Assistant Coach Duane Heck** (1968 Bluebook)

Newfolden Coach **Ron Ueland** offers history on District 32: *When I returned to coach at Newfolden the fall of 1967, Jim Musburger was generally regarded as the premier coach in District 32. AJ Kramer had retired at Roseau, Art Anderson at Baudette, and Jim Schindele at Stephen. Jerry Snyder had left Middle River for Lake City and Frank Konoutek at Newfolden, for Sebeka. Louis Deere had just returned to Kennedy and Warren Keller had not yet come to Argyle. Jim Musburger was the guy for a young coach to look to for a role model. Due to the make-up of the district, we did not automatically play Karlstad during the regular season. Each subdistrict was a conference. The West (Northern Lights) consisted of Argyle, Stephen, Kennedy, Hallock, Humboldt, Lancaster, Lake Bronson, Karlstad and Strandquist. The East (North Border) was Baudette, Williams, Warroad, Roseau, Badger, Greenbush, Middle River and Newfolden. Williams was soon to consolidate with Baudette but Grygla built a high school and was added. You played each team in your conference twice and were limited to eighteen games. That did not offer many opportunities to play someone from the other subdistrict. I asked Jim about scheduling a game the* *following year. He was intimidating to say the least but always very kind and helpful to me and I believe to all of the younger coaches he came in contact with. Though in those early years, Karlstad always beat us, it was never as bad as it could have been as he always pulled his starters and kept the game respectable. The first game I coached against Jim was the District 32 tournament in 1968. Our principal – A.D. had already told me we had little chance against Musburger's team! He was right. Our offense didn't work at all. Their defenders wouldn't cooperate and follow us to where we could set screens. It seemed as though we played one against five all game. It was a long night.*

*We finally beat Karlstad in the 1972 District semi-final. We won on a last second shot – one of those lucky wins. Jim came to our locker room right after the game congratulating our coaches and players, shaking hands and wishing us good luck in the finals. He was as gracious in defeat as he had always been in victory. In 1977, we won our first District 32 championship, again he was the first to offer congratulations and support in the upcoming regional tournament.*

*I always had a great deal of respect and admiration for Jim as did all of the coaches. When he spoke at District 32 meetings, he commanded everyone's attention. His ideas carried a lot of weight. Jim's teams were always well behaved, disciplined, fundamentally sound and played excellent defense. Defense in the 50s and 60s was usually man to man, which meant that you stuck to your assigned man all game. You literally picked him up when he got off the bus and harassed him till it was time to leave and he got back on. It made screening defenders away from the ball relatively easy. The other type of defense was a zone where each player guarded an area of the court. Jim's defense incorporated some of each. In his defense, you guarded your man when he had the ball and when he didn't, you guarded the basket.*

*For the next 30 years I had some success using that defense. As time went by, I attended clinics and read books. I heard Bobby Knight talk about help defense and how and where to move when the ball moves. Bobby must have learned that from Jim Musburger. Today when you hear television announcers talking about help side defense and defensive rotation, why, Jim Musburger was doing it in Northwestern Minnesota 60 years ago!*

**1968 Sub-District All-Conference Players: The coaches chose the following All-Conference team left to right (back row): Tom and David Kujava, Strandquist; Glen Schmidt, Conrad Lubarski, Argyle; Arden Jergenson, Wayne Halfmann, Stephen. Front row: Randy Nordin, Lancaster; Lee Jerome, Humboldt; Brian Sjodin, Karlstad; Dean Carlson, Charles Trolin, Hallock; Don Grundstrom, Kennedy.** (21 March 1968, *Karlstad Advocate*)

**Dick Moen** joined Heck and Musburger as assistant coach for the 1968 football season. Led by co-captains Greg Oistad and Mike Folland, the team boasted a 5-3 record. All-conference selections were Brian Sjodin, Mike Folland and John Nelson.

**John Nelson '68** shared his thoughts: *Mr. Musburger and Mr. Heck complimented each other the way they worked together. The Rabbits were very lucky to have them. My senior year was '68 and we had a great bunch of guys who all wanted the best for the team. We* *accomplished more than what some thought we could, but we gave it all we had.  Mr. Musburger would write on the chalkboard, "When the going gets tough, the tough get going."  That phrase has followed me throughout life.*

**1967-68 Football Team:  Front row:  Brian Sjodin, John Nelson, Mike Folland, Paul Farbo, Greg Johnson, Lowell Sjodin, Kent Hanson, Greg Oistad, Chuck Johnson, Jan Nordin, Steve Andersen. Back row:  Coach Heck, Coach Musburger, John Oistad, Jon Nordine, Stuart Spilde, James Falk, Jack Oistad, Leon Thompson, Doug Larson, Robert Clark, Leland Netterlund, Tim Vagle, Scott Falk, manager, Coach Moen, Jerry Stallock, manager.**
(1968 Bluebook)

**Varsity cheerleaders:  Priscilla Erickson, Janakaye Dagen, Sheila Nordine, Jill Musburger, Peggy Johnson** (1968 Bluebook)

## 13.  KARLSTAD RABBITS 1968-69

*I remember Kennedy coach Louis Deere standing by the end of the gym as we were beating Argyle.  Kennedy could not beat them but we could.  He was cheering us on to victory.* – Lowell Sjodin '70

The 1969 Varsity Basketball season opened without a senior on the team and still wound up in third place in the Northern Lights Conference behind Kennedy and Argyle who each lost one game during the season.  This surprising and exciting team, coached by Jim Musburger and Dick Moen, took Karlstad to the District 32 tournament where the Rabbits upset Argyle 57-54 to advance to the finals before falling to Kennedy 59-39.

**Karlstad Varsity Basketball Team 1968-1969:  Kneeling:  Lowell Sjodin, (captain).  Standing left to right:  John Oistad, Glen Spilde, Stuart Spilde, Jim Musburger, Steve Spilde, Kent Hanson, Jerry Pietruszewski, Jerry Kuznia, Richie Pietruszewski, Chris Johnson, Harlan Bengtson.** (1969 Bluebook)

Captain Lowell Sjodin earned a place on the All-Conference team. Student managers Matthew Berg and Leland Netterlund took care of all the team details, while cheerleaders Jill Musburger, Margo Dagen,

Colleen Koland, Diedre Pederson, Denise Sjodin and Loretta Olson led the crowd spirit.

**Lowell Sjodin** remembers 1969 as the year Karlstad could not defeat the formidable Kennedy Rockets led by Ron Visness, Robert Eukel, Ron Peterson, Karl Urbaniak and Randy Swanberg: *We lost to Kennedy four times that year: twice during the year, once in the sub-district and again in district finals to region. We did beat Argyle in the district as they defeated Kennedy during the year and were favored to go to the region. It was a good win, but I always felt bad for Lubarski of Argyle – he was a class act and always a challenge to play against. Coach came up with a game plan to beat them and it worked just like he planned. I remember Louis Deere standing by the end of the gym as we were beating Argyle. Kennedy could not beat them but we could. He was cheering us on to victory.*

Argyle's **Conrad Lubarski** recalls the Karlstad-Argyle game: *As Lowell Sjodin said, "Coach Musburger had a good game plan and it worked." I remember Karlstad had an almost perfect third quarter offensively and built a good lead. We cut the margin in the final quarter but lost. That Karlstad team was mainly juniors and underclassmen. Our hope to play Kennedy, who we defeated in the Sub-District Championship, for a trip to the region was spoiled. Kennedy defeated Karlstad. Kennedy was a very worthy district representative with the likes of Ron Peterson, Bob Eukel, Ron Visness, Karl Urbaniak, Mark Kraulik, Randy Swanberg and others. The Kennedy coach was another memorable and successful basketball icon of northwestern Minnesota, Louis Deere.*

Argyle assistant coach **John Schmidt** would scout surrounding teams: *Karlstad was well coached, well-disciplined and had excellent defense. Jim Musburger was the first coach in our area to practice with the A and B teams together so both teams were doing the same thing. We copied that strategy from Karlstad.*

Kennedy was tough that year but guarding Lowell was equally daunting. Teammate **Steve Spilde'70** shared an experience: *Over the years, I have occasionally recalled something Coach said in practice that I thought was kind of funny then, and still do. I had the thankless task of*

90

defending against Lowell Sjodin as the team worked on a play for him. Lowell pivoted to his left the first couple of run-throughs, so I cheated that way on defense the next time. Coach blew his whistle and "gently" advised Lowell not to go the same direction every time, saying (about me) "he'll figure it out, the guy's an A student, well, potentially."

**Jimmy Musburger '72,** the coach's son, describes the talented Kennedy team: *I was a freshman and played B-squad and sat on the bench for varsity games. We had a good team, but Kennedy had one of those teams that came along once in a coach's career. They were talented and deep. We were young and I don't recall many seniors on that team. We battled Kennedy but they were too talented. I'm sure we won a majority of our games that year. Once again, we were the team that coaches feared because we were fundamentally sound and had great coaching. Dad created a culture where we expected to win and believed we could beat anybody.*

**Coach Musburger** chimes in: *Kennedy was always tough. In my early years of coaching, brothers Lynden and Wayne Langen and twin brothers Vince and Virgil Sonju were great ball players. Louis Deere and I had a great rivalry and friendship that continued until I retired.*

**Louis Deere, Kennedy Coach ( 1965-2000)**

**May 13, 1939 – June 21, 2009**

According to **Lowell Sjodin**, Coach Musburger softened the referees for tournament play: *When it got close to tournament time, Coach would have the refs that were hired for the tournament ref a game of ours. We had to be on our best behavior no matter the call. I can still see him standing as calm as can be telling us to raise our hands when a foul was called on us. The coaches and players from the other team didn't seem to catch on and would complain. We would go into the tournament with the respect of those refs. He was always thinking ahead for any advantage. I remember when we played Strandquist at home and Coach would turn up the heat figuring they were out of shape and wanting them to sweat a little extra.* (Kent Hanson reported that Coach Musburger believed that Coach Deere turned up the heat in Kennedy when Karlstad played there).

*Here's another memory. At the start of the basketball season, coach would sit us all down on the bleachers and go over the rules. If you got caught drinking, you were done for the season. Smoking was two weeks according to Minnesota High School League, but he treated that the same as drinking and you were done for the year. I don't think any of us ever got in those situations.*

*He also did not like people coming in to watch us practice so he would take jump ropes and tie the gym doors shut. We watched the superintendent stick his hands through and untie it. It took him quite a while. This was very entertaining for the team. Whenever we played against a taller player, coach would call on Karl Carlson, the music teacher, to suit up for practice. One of Coach's favorite saying was "chickens one day and feathers the next," – this usually meant he was in a good mood and enjoying the practice.*

**Lowell** also recalled playing Stephen at Kennedy in the 1969 sub-district tournament: *We were tied at the end of the game and they had a turnover and scoffed up the ball. Coach called a timeout. It took him about five seconds to tell us what he wanted us to do. We all just stood there not saying a word. I remember looking over at the Stephen huddle and they were listening intently to their coach. Some of the players were looking at us just standing there, but we already had our instructions and knew exactly what to do. In short, coach said, bring the ball up, Lowell break to the top of the circle, pass the ball to Lowell,*

Kent break across the middle. Lowell, pass the ball to Kent. Kent put the ball in the basket. This is what he said, and this is what we did, and this is how we won that game. I can still see those Stephen players looking at our huddle and wondering what we were thinking just standing there and not saying a word after five seconds. Kent Hanson tossed in a fielder with 19 seconds to give Karlstad a 55-54 win over Stephen and ended up with 22 points for the game. Terry Laudal scored 19 for Stephen.

Kennedy's **Ken Urbaniak '67** relates a story from 1969: *Louis Deere told me that at the end of the conference year, the coaches held a meeting to select an All-Conference team. Kennedy and Argyle tied for first place and four players from each team qualified for the team. Deere nominated Ron Peterson, Bob Eukel, Ron Visness and Karl Urbaniak for the team, but the Argyle coach refused to vote for Karl. Jim Musburger fought for Karl and let the Argyle coach have it from all sides, but he would not budge. So Louis nominated Randy Swanberg, his 6th man, and he made the all-conference team.*

Assistant coach **Dick Moen** remembers teaching in Karlstad his first year: *First and foremost, Jim Musburger was a professional. His dedication to teaching was so intense. Every day he would be in early and prepare. He was a good influence on Mr. Gerald Hanson and Mr. Moen in our first year out. Once he referred to Karlstad and Halma as "Mecca and Medina," the two holy cities of Saudi Arabia!*

*We did not have tall players but through physical steps and object lessons, he could somehow make a team click. It was practice, practice and practice. Sticking to basics yielded dividends in many close games. Defense won the game. One game Louis Deere of Kennedy set up a hutch and threw some carrots and lettuce on the gym floor. It helped the eyes of the Rabbits as we shot well over 50%!*

*Somebody said he was the laziest man in town in the summer (save for lawn mowing) but the hardest working teacher and coach from September to May.*

*One time we had the van full of players as we headed down to the state tournament. Principal Earl Lutz and Superintendent Henry Martin were watching in the window and as I pulled out, I hit the accelerator TOO hard and blew snow and mud all over. I remember how Jim covered his eyes. Down at the Hampton Arms Hotel in Minneapolis, Steve Spilde knocked on our door at 7 a.m. and in a deep bass voice announced, "Mr. Moen, I think I have been hit by a car." I'll never forget how Jim, still in bed, pulled the sheets over his head. We told Steve, "Do not call home, but take two aspirins!" Those were the days.*

**Assistant Coach Dick Moen, Captain Lowell Sjodin, Coach Jim Musburger** (1969 Bluebook)

Captains Jan Nordin and Steve Andersen led the varsity football team to a season record 3 wins, 5 losses by defeating Lancaster, Newfolden and Oslo. The varsity roster included: David Olson, Jerry Olson, Lowell Sjodin, Dan Flint, Stuart Spilde, Paul Farbo, Kent Hanson, Leland Netterlund, Doug Larson, Robert Nelson, Ron Bengtson, John Erickson, Glen Spilde, John Oistad, Harlan Bengtson, David Gorsuch, Jon Nordine, Mark Prosser, Jimmy Musburger, Jerry Kuznia, Lamar

Gunnarson and manager Tom Stallock. Jerry Hanson joined the coaching staff assisted by Jim Musburger. Steve Andersen, Leland Netterlund and Lowell Sjodin received All-Conference honors.

**Jan Nordin '69** shares favorite memories: *We were preparing to play Argyle, and Coach said we needed to be tough for this game because Argyle had really strong players. He said he was out for a drive and ended up over by Argyle and wasn't sure of where he was. He saw a young farmer working in a field, so he stopped to ask for directions. It happened to be Conrad Lubarski. Coach asked which way to town and Conrad picked up the plow and pointed "that-a-way!" Another memory is when we practiced twice a day in August for football, and I would lead warm-ups. We did leg raises and Coach decided to randomly walk around and step on our stomachs. That really got our attention, as he was not a small guy! When I watch the Minnesota State basketball tournament, it seems that most teams could benefit by one of Coach M's basic basketball rules. NO CROSS COURT PASSES!! EVER!!*

**Karlstad Varsity Football Team 1969: Kneeling left to right: D. Olson, J. Olson, L. Sjodin, D. Flint, S. Spilde, J. Nordin (Capt.), S. Andersen (Capt.), P. Farbo, K. Hanson, L. Netterlund, D. Larson, R. Nelson. Standing: Coach Hanson, T. Stallock, manager, R. Bengtson, J. Erickson, G. Spilde, J. Oistad, H. Bengtson, D. Gorsuch, J. Nordine, M. Prosser, J. Musburger, J. Kuznia, L. Gunnarson, Coach Musburger.** (1969 Bluebook)

# 14. KARLSTAD RABBITS 1969-70

*I remember the look on Coach Musburger's face during the win against Hallock in Hallock in 1968, the win against Argyle in Stephen in 1969, and the 1970 win in Stephen against Stephen in a packed house. I will always remember that big smile and his grin from ear to ear.* – Jerry Pietruszewski '70

The year 1970 was a banner year for the Rabbits. All the veteran players returned including seniors Stuart Spilde, Jerry Pietruszewski, Lowell Sjodin (captain), Chris Johnson and Harlan Bengtson; juniors John Oistad, Richie Pietruszewski, Kent Hanson, Glen Spilde, and sophomores Jimmy Musburger and Jerry Olson, coached by Jim Musburger and George Bunn. Seniors Leland Netterlund and Neal Benson managed the team.

**Karlstad Rabbits Varsity Team 1969-70: J. Erickson, J. Oistad, S. Spilde, R. Pietruszewski, J. Musburger, L. Sjodin, K. Hanson, J. Olson, C. Johnson, G. Spilde, H. Bengtson. Absent: Jerry Pietruszewski** (1970 Bluebook)

Stephen captured the conference title with a perfect 14-0 season followed by Karlstad with a 12-2 record, both losses to Stephen. During sub-district play, the Rabbits crushed Humboldt 78-32 and Argyle 67-58 before falling to the Stephen Tigers 54 to 43 for the championship. Jerry Pietruszewski and Kent Hanson each scored 13 points against the Tigers. After losing to Stephen twice in conference play and again in the sub-districts, the Rabbits defeated the Tigers in the district tournament to advance to the regionals in Grand Forks. Jerry Pietruszewski, Lowell Sjodin and Chris Johnson were named All-Conference. At the regional tournament, the Rabbits lost 53-51 to a tough Mentor team with Kent Hanson tossing in 22 points. Alvarado also prevailed 56-50 with Lowell Sjodin adding 20 points.

**Jerry Pietruszewski '70** voices his varsity experience: *It was memorable and we always learned to play basketball the right way. Coach's emphasis was always to play defense and when I look back, he had some good ones. He always said, "Don't run with your back to the ball, because you might get hit in the back of your head." That was his cardinal sin in basketball.*

*I remember being on the bench my sophomore year with Stuart and Jerry Kuznia and watching Brian, Jack Oistad, Greg Oistad, John Nelson, Lowell and Craig Spilde. We had a pretty good team but Hallock had the best one and were the favorites, but we beat Hallock on their own floor to win the sub-district championship. Being there to celebrate with them was really something!*

*Coach Musburger had that way of getting you to play hard especially on defense and rebounding the ball. I remember a time in our junior year when we had no seniors on our team and Argyle and Kennedy were the good teams. We weren't expected to do much except be competitive. We couldn't beat Kennedy or Argyle during the season, but played Argyle in the district. We went to the locker room at halftime and Daryl Peterson, all conference, was having a good first half, and my brother Richie was guarding him. Coach Musburger was letting him have it from all sides. We came out in the second half, shut down Peterson, and of course, Lowell also did a good job on Connie Lubarski, and won the game.*

*It was sort of ironic because that year it was supposed to be Kennedy and Argyle to play in the District Championship, but here we were playing Kennedy. They went on to play in the region only to lose to Thief River Falls on a last second shot by Sheldon Joppru at the UND*

*Fieldhouse. Kennedy thanked us that year for beating Argyle in the district as they had lost to Argyle twice during the season and once in the sub-district championship. But once again, it was Coach Musburger getting us to play hard defense.*

*Our senior year, Karlstad, Kennedy, Stephen and Argyle were the teams to beat. We beat Kennedy and Argyle but couldn't beat Stephen. We lost to them three times but finally beat them in the District Championship at Stephen. The place was packed and some of the fans sat on chairs on the edge of the floor.*

*Reflecting on it now, I remember the look on Coach Musburger's face during the win against Hallock in Hallock in 1968, the win against Argyle in Stephen in 1969, and the 1970 win in Stephen against Stephen in a packed house. I will always remember that big smile and his grin from ear to ear. I also remember traveling to Bemidji on Saturday after narrowly beating Strandquist the night before. Then we beat Bemidji and had to be escorted out of the building.*

*It was always something to watch Coach Musburger, Louis Deere, Jim Schindele and Warren Keller from Argyle. They were all fierce coaches but they had such mutual respect for one another and were all such great friends. It was really something to be a part of this in my life. I think the biggest thing that we took from coach is that we all became better men in life after graduation. When Lowell, Kent, Richie, John Oistad, Glen and I get together, somehow the conversation gets back to basketball and Coach Jim Musburger.*

**Chris Johnson '70** reflects on his senior year: *I hurt my back at the beginning of the season, could not make a layup and did not start on the basketball team until after the Argyle game. Once I started, I had some great games scoring 19 against Kennedy, 17 against Humboldt, 12 against Strandquist and 7 in the Bemidji game. I only played five minutes in the District championship game but I made two big free throws to help win the game. Lowell had hurt his knee so Jimmy helped out tremendously that game.*

*I loved every minute of basketball practice and was the last person off the court after every practice. I was used to working hard on the farm, and practice was so much fun for me. We would compete in free throw practice – I shot 50 % but Lowell shot 82%. He was quiet and confident. I also loved my coach and when he told me to do something, I did it. I was going to carry out everything he said. We knew that with our coach, we had a good chance of pulling out every game, no matter who he put in the game. By the way, I wore out a jump rope that year.*

**1970 West Sub-District All-Conference at Stephen: (Front) Chris Johnson, Jerry Pietruszewski, Lowell Sjodin, Mike Knoll, Dave Sundby (back) Randy Swanberg, Terry Swanson, Karl Urbaniak, Phil Chwialkowski, Lynn Safranski, Mike Stoltman, Ron Jensen**
(5 March 1970, p. 6 *North Star News*)

**District 32 Champs Seniors with Trophy: Jerry Pietruszewski, Lowell Sjodin, Harlan Bengtson, Chris Johnson, Stuart Spilde**
(12 March 1970 p. 5 *North Star News*)

**1970 District 32 Champions** (12 March 1970, *North Star News*)

Kennedy's **Ken Urbaniak '67** remembers when Lowell hurt his knee in the championship game against Stephen: *After Lowell hurt his knee, Coach Musburger would travel with Lowell and Kent to Kennedy for whirlpool treatments. We had an old whirlpool from the Air Force that looked like a cow trough. Coach Louis Deere told me that he and Jim Musburger spent a lot of time together during the whirlpool treatments and became good friends. I also remember that Musburger never ran up the score against a weaker team.*

**Lowell** responds: *Louis Deere offered the whirlpool to us. Ken's brother, Karl, and Ron Jenson from Stephen were the two toughest people I played against in high school. Karl played baseball and football at Minot State where they retired his number. Karl was then drafted by Chicago in the United States Football League. Kennedy was a good rivalry and always a class act – just really nice people.*

The Rabbits lost just four games in non-tournament play: twice to Stephen 65-59 and 45-42, East Grand Forks 60-56 and East Grand Forks Sacred Heart 55-54. Although all the games were close, **Jimmy Musburger '72** vividly recalls the game they lost to East Grand Forks by four points: *Larry Selk was the EGF coach and they had one of the most talented teams in the state. Their front line was 6'8", 6'7" and 6'5". They had two talented guards in Kurt Knoff and Scott Gravseth and Joe Monda played center. Knoff played safety for the Minnesota Vikings and ended his career there. We had them beat except for seriously poor officiating.*

**Coach Musburger** answers: *Two Grand Forks officials officiated and they did not like me. They refereed several of our games in the past and always did a poor job. When we played Alvarado in our second regional tournament, some kid from Alvarado ran over Ernie and the same ref called it on Ernie. George Bunn got mad and I had to restrain him.*

Sportswriter **Bob Lyons** wrote about East Grand Forks coach Larry Selk's reaction to the game: *Green Wave coach Larry Selk was both awed by Karlstad's shooting and Monda's performance (29 points). Of Karlstad he said, "I've never seen better shooting from the outside. Of course we didn't put enough pressure on their shooters, but I just couldn't believe it. We kept expecting them to cool off, but they didn't."*

Lowell Sjodin scored 17 points to lead the way while Richie Pietruszewski added 15 points, Jerry Pietruszewski scored 14, Chris Johnson 7 and Kent Hanson 3.

**John Oistad '71** echoes two memorable events from 1970: *One game I will always remember was when we went to Bemidji and beat them 55 – 49. We had to be escorted to the bus after the game as some rowdy Bemidji fans lined the sidewalk waiting for us because they weren't very happy that a small school had beaten the bigger Lumberjacks! I will never forget beating Stephen in 1970 for the District Title in their new gym! Then practicing and playing in the Region Tourney at Hyslop in Grand Forks and staying at the Westward Ho because it was storming. Great memories.*

Bemidji sportswriter **Cliff Morlan** wrote about the Karlstad vs. Bemidji game in the *Bemidji Pioneer: Saturday, a hustling Karlstad quintet, coached by ex-lumberjack Jim Musburger, ran Bemidji into the ground with a first quarter barrage behind the final scoring of Lowell Sjodin. The blonde forward threw in 14 points as the Rabbits jumped to a 20-13 lead and never trailed. Sjodin ended with 24 points to pace both teams while Pietruszewski had 11. Karlstad held a wide 43-31 lead off the boards paced by Pietruszewski's nine. The Karlstad B squad also won 42-40 paced by Jim Musburger, son of the varsity coach.*

Apparently both the Sjodin boys were asked to leave the gym, but it took Lowell longer to get back in. **Lowell "Stretch" Sjodin** recalls: *I remember when I was in 7th grade practicing with the varsity and not giving my best and was told in a very clear way to get out of his gym. I left and did not get back in till the next year. I was ready to pay attention then. Our practices were very serious but also a lot of fun. We heard many lectures ranging from the Roman Empire to present days at that time. I was in 8th grade and I remember walking home from school and coach came up to me and said he was counting on me next year. I said, who me, and he said, yes, you. Coach is a very special person in my life. When Kent Hanson and I get together, we go over all the good times playing sports together and Musburger always comes up. He has been a big part of our lives and we judge other coaches simply by saying that is not how Musburger would do it. When I was in 8th grade on the B team, I broke my arm and had to learn to make layups with my left arm.*

*I went up for a rebound and a big Kuznia from Argyle grabbed the ball, swung me around, and I landed on my right elbow. That really hurt and I couldn't straighten out my right arm. I wore a cast on my right arm and that is how I learned to use my left arm in basketball. My first game on the B team, I had a good game with lots of rebounds. Wherever the ball went, I went after it. Coach was impressed and came into the locker room and said you're dressing for varsity. I have not forgotten that moment in all these years.*

**Tim Olson** gives a nod to Lowell's story: *I kind of remember the part of Lowell getting kicked out of the gym when he was young. Faintly. But lesson learned, huh? You don't mess with the boss, the top dog, the biggest bull, the toughest lion. He wasn't the only one that was taught a lesson in life.*

**Lowell** went on to play for Mayville State College after high school: *Mayville Coach Doug Eiken ran a motion offense, a lot of moving from one spot to the next. He put me at point guard but I was too slow and couldn't dribble. I couldn't keep up to the smaller guards, but could handle the guys bigger than me up to a point. Coach Musburger taught us how to box out and get position to rebound. Eiken would tell the rest of the team to watch me. I would get position and let the ball hit the floor and then grab it just like Coach Musburger taught us. When I was at Mayville, we would head to the locker room at half-time. I didn't understand why it took the coach so long to come into the locker room. In high school, we would head to the music room. Coach Musburger had a big blackboard set up. He would walk right in and start breaking down the first half. What we did right or wrong. He didn't have to stand outside and talk to anybody else to figure out what to do. He was always in control and gave us the confidence in ourselves to go back and win the game. He wasn't a holler guy, he didn't have to be, he had our attention. I remember when coach came to practice and if he didn't change into his practice outfit and was still in his suit, it was going to be a very serious practice.*

Teammate **Harlan Bengtson'70** echoes Lowell's remarks: *What comes to the forefront for me were Coach's chalk talks. He was really good at preparing us before the game and at halftime. He would break down what the other team was doing and what we needed to change or* *continue. Coach was very smart about the X's and O's of offense and defense, game planning and more importantly on making adjustments as the game dictated. I looked forward to the casual scrimmages and shooting around.*

**Gary Schuler,** assistant basketball coach in Kennedy, recalls 1970: *I started my teaching and coaching career in 1970 in Kennedy under Coach Louis C. Deere. It was a great way to start in this profession. I can remember Coach Deere detailing the two rivalries that were at the top of his list. They were the Karlstad Rabbits and the Stephen Tigers. My first trip to play the Rabbits was quite an eye-opening event. The gym rocked as fans anticipated a great basketball game. I was only in Kennedy two years but to watch how both teams relied on defense and fundamentals led to a lot of my coaching philosophy in my 31-year head-coaching career.*

*One ironic twist as I saw it. I left Kennedy to coach sophomores at Grand Forks Red River in 1972-73. The head coaching position opened and I applied. I had a long extensive interview with the AD, school board and superintendent. I didn't hear for a short while, but then was offered the job. I found out that I was their third choice behind Louis Deere and Jim Musburger. They both said no and stayed in Kennedy and Karlstad respectively. I should have thanked both of them as our family still calls Warren home.*

**Neal Benson '70** remembers when Coach Musburger recruited him for team manager: *I joined Leland Netterlund my senior year as student manager of the basketball team. It was a magical opportunity for me and I am grateful to Coach for taking me under his wing where I learned discipline, organization and dedication to principles. Coach got blazers with a rabbit embroidered on the pocket, and I was so proud to wear that blazer and arrive at a visitor or tournament site as a team. Great fun to hang out with Lowell, Kuz, Pete and my drumming mate, Harlan – they treated me like a teammate.*

**B Team 1970: Row 1:  T. Anderson, R. Bengtson, J. Musburger, M. Sang, J. Olson, J. Erickson, R. Johnson.  Row 2:  M. Berg, manager; D. Grandstrand, T. Johnson, C. Bolin, J. Anderson, D. Renstrom, Coach Bunn** (1970 Bluebook)

Led by seniors Lowell Sjodin, Harlan Bengtson, Mark Prosser, Doug Larson (co-captain), Stuart Spilde (co-captain), Robert Nelson, Leland Netterlund and Danny Flint, the talented athletes of '70 went undefeated in football to win the conference.

**1970 Seniors:  Lowell Sjodin, Harlan Bengtson, Mark Prosser, Doug Larson, Stuart Spilde, Bob Nelson, Leland Netterlund, Danny Flint** (1970 Bluebook)

## Undefeated 1969-70 Conference Champions

Row 1: Tim Lutz, Asst. Manager; Mark Prosser, Kent Hanson, Harlan Bengtson, Doug Larson, Stuart Spilde, Lowell Sjodin, Leland Netterlund, Robert Nelson, Dan Flint. Row 2: Terry Anderson, Dean Johnson, John Erickson, Don Johnson, Jim Musburger, Jerry Olson, David Peterson, David Olson, John Oistad. Row 3: Coach Musburger, Kent Benson, James Anderson, Dave Vik, Earl Gorsuch, Gus Berggren, David Gorsuch, Ron Bengtson, Jon Nordine, Student Manager; Coach Hanson. Absent: **G. Spilde** (1970 Bluebook)

All-Conference team players were Stuart Spilde, Leland Netterlund, Lowell Sjodin, Danny Flint, Kent Hanson and Doug Larson.

**Doug Larson '70** sums up football practice: *My most fun memories are coach giving us water during practice and pretending to step on our stomach during calisthenics. For water break, we had gallon jugs. In order not to drink from the jug and share germs, Coach Musburger took great delight to pour a dose directly into our gullet as we gathered around him like a bunch of baby birds, all with our mouths open. One exercise we would do is leg raisers. Coach would walk around while we lay on our backs with our legs raised a few inches. He would pretend that he was going to step on our stomachs only to step over us without putting any weight on that leg. It was his way to play with us and cause us to tense up thinking we had to support his weight.*

**All- Conference:  Leland Netterlund, Danny Flint, Doug Larson, Stuart Spilde, Lowell Sjodin, Kent Hanson** (1970 Bluebook)

**Varsity cheerleaders 1969-70:  Margo Dagen, Diedre Pederson, Chrystal Johnson, Jill Musburger, Denise Sjodin, Colleen Koland**
(from the files of Jill Musburger Johnson)

**Diedre Pederson Nordin '71** shared an off-court memory: *When I took driver's training from Mr. Musburger, he picked up Margo Dagen, Tim Vagle, and me at our homes in the country. He said he liked training "farm kids" because they already had driving experience and didn't get the jitters like some of the "town kids" did. We were pretty proud of that! Then one day, Tim asked him how he got his teams to win every year. He told Tim that he looked to see what skills his players had and planned his coaching around their talents. He said if a coach just uses the same plan every year, the team won't win every year. As your players change, you need to adjust your strategy. I have never forgotten that. Maximizing the talent you are given is the key to success.*

**B Team Cheerleaders: Leanne Folland, Cindy Vik, Pam Boen, Sue Oien** (1970 Bluebook)

# 15. KARLSTAD RABBITS 1970-71

*We had white high-top tennis shoes that had to be polished the night before every game. If you missed and Coach saw it, you did not play. We also had to wear white undershorts as well as a jockstrap – this was so we wouldn't stain the white uniforms that were so damn tight if you farted, it wouldn't leave until the game was over and you undressed.* – Kent Hanson '71

The 1971 varsity basketball season opened with a crushing win over Hallock 84-45. The Rabbits went on to defeat Roseau and Mentor before East Grand Forks thumped the Rabbits 99-64, followed by a heartbreaking loss to Kennedy 46-45. Karlstad prevailed in the next ten games before falling to Argyle 69-67. The sub-district tournament was eliminated that year and the two top teams in the East, (Greenbush, Badger, Middle River, Newfolden, Roseau, Baudette, Warroad), and the top two teams in the West, (Karlstad, Kennedy, Hallock, Humboldt, Stephen, Argyle, Lancaster), were seeded into the District 32 tournament. The boys of '71 took 3rd place in the district by downing Baudette 86-58 before losing to the formidable Kennedy Rockets 67-61 in the second game and narrowly defeating Argyle 70-65 for consolation honors.

The varsity team, led by seniors Richie Pietruszewski and Kent Hanson (co-captains), Glen Spilde, and John Oistad, included Jim Musburger, Jerry Olson, John Erickson, David Vik, Mark Seng, Tim Johnson, Bob Johnson, and managers Matt Berg and David Peterson. West Sub-district 32 All-Conference selections were Jim Musburger, Richie Pietruszewski and Kent Hanson.

**John Oistad '71** recalls basketball practice: *One of the things that I remember about Coach Musburger was his attention to detail and fundamentals. All the drills that we did every day in practice (passing, dribbling, screen & roll, boxing out, 3 on 2; and how they were incorporated into our offense) helped make us one of the best teams in the area. I also remember how competitive our practices were. Coach made sure that our out of district schedule allowed us to play some of the better bigger schools in the area such as Bemidji, East Grand Forks, and Thief River.*

Karlstad Rabbits Varsity Team: 1970-71: Row 1: G. Spilde, J. Musburger, R. Pietruszewski, K. Hanson, J. Olson, J. Oistad. Row 2: M. Berg, manager, J. Erickson, D. Vik, M. Seng, T. Johnson, B. Johnson, D. Peterson, manager. (1971 Bluebook)

**Kent Hanson '71** elaborates on practice details: *I do remember that you would never want to have turnovers, make a bad pass, take a bad shot, and for god's sake, not hustle. A must was to take the baseline away, block out on rebounds, ball fake, shoot with arch, follow your shot, cut off the cutters through the lane, don't dribble too much, roll the right way off a screen, fight through all screens, get a hand in the shooter's face and I could go on and on. He would quote, "Rome wasn't built in a day," and "the mind is willing but the body is weak." I remember when I was a sophomore and we played a jamboree in Argyle. Coach knew that he had to keep the two Polacks right behind each other so they wouldn't go up for a lay-up during warm-ups and run into each other. Well, guess what? They got separated and did exactly that – met in midair and fell to the ground. Coach just shook his head.*

*Do you remember the cool dark blue suits we wore with dark blue shirts and white ties? Reminds me of the Blues Brothers. Oh and how about this! We had white high-top tennis shoes that had to be polished the night before every game. If you missed and he saw it, you did not play. We also had to wear white undershorts as well as a jockstrap – this was* so we wouldn't stain the white uniforms that were so damn tight if you farted, it wouldn't leave until the game was over and you undressed. How about the Bugs Bunny on our warm up jackets? Haircuts, yes by all means, and never miss practice or be late. More, as a daily routine for practice, we sprayed tough skin on our feet, then put lube on our feet to prevent blisters. We also took two vitamin C tablets to prevent a cold. Then Mr. Musburger gave us salt tablets, and he had us fooled into believing the salt would prevent us from losing too much water during practice and games, but as I got older, I think it was saltpeter, so we wouldn't have interest in girls. We also had a small glass of coke at half time. Right at the final pregame huddle, he would always say a 'small prayer' that no one would get hurt and all would have a good game. Then he would snap that smelling salt, we all took a sniff which was strong, and away we would go.

Also, he definitely wanted to win the County Seats: Hallock, Roseau and Thief River Falls. We ran a sagging man-to-man defense and it was a treat for Coach to watch if the other team would run a zone offense against us thinking we were in a zone.

When I started coaching, I got to be friends with Deere, Keller and Ueland, three life-long successful coaches and they shared a common comment in concert – when you played a Musburger coached team, you knew they were going to be the toughest team to beat, not because they had the better players or team, but because they played the best defense, didn't turn the ball over, and you didn't get second shots because they blocked so well for rebounds. Force other teams to take bad shots (lower percentage), don't allow a second shot (rebound well) and if you don't have many turnovers, you maximize your number of attempts. Most of my younger coaching peers could never figure this out, shit, my teams could beat better ones just because of those three focuses.

Coach Musburger could have coached forever and been successful year in and year out. Coach was very good to me and I would use all that he taught me when I coached, and it has stood the test of time. He was a disciplinarian for sure, but I loved him for it. He saved me from being basically a bad person.

**Richie Pietruszewski '71** laments their desire to advance to the state tournament: *Coach Musburger was respected by all of us that played for him. His discipline was our success. Back then in 1969-1971, he was like a second dad to me. I remember us jumping rope at a fast pace every practice for a long period of time, which was one of many exercises that kept us in excellent shape. Most enjoyable practices were playing against Thief River Falls, and favorite games were against Bemidji, East Grand Forks, Middle River and of course, all tournament games. Just wish we could have gone to the state tourney once for Coach. We will always respect him, and still call him Coach Musburger.*

**1971 Co-captains Richie Pietruszewski and Kent Hanson with Coach Musburger** (1971 Bluebook)

**Seniors: J. Oistad, R. Pietruszewski, K. Hanson, G. Spilde** (1971 Bluebook)

**John Erickson '72** shares life on the B team that year: *In 1971, Jimmy, John Oistad, Kent Hanson, Glen Spilde, Jerry Olson and Richie Pietruszewski had another good year. While they won most of the A team games, Coach had several of us who were juniors play B team games. We were probably not the most talented group, but I think Coach knew that we were all he would have (except for Jimmy) next year, so we needed the work. It was fun. George Bunn coached us to a one-loss season.*

*Before every game, we gathered in our disease-infected locker room where Mr. Bunn would have us touch a ball and tell us, "Shake the hell out of this and win!" I remember a banner in Mr. Bunn's classroom, "Bunn's Bunnies are the Best!" The guys on that B team included: Tim Anderson, Ken Johnson, Dan Sandahl, Denal Grahn, Lee Sele, Ricky Netterlund, John Erickson, David Grandstrand, David Vik, Robert Johnson, Mark Seng, Bobby Johnson, Tim Johnson and managers Matt Berg and Keith Olson. Mr. Bunn and Mr. Musburger were a great team.*

**B Team 1970-71: Front Row: Terry Anderson, Ken Johnson, Dan Sandahl, Denal Grahn, Lee Sele, Ricky Netterlund. Back Row: Matt Berg, John Erickson, Tim Johnson, Mark Sang, David Grandstrand, David Vik, Robert Johnson, Keith Olson, Coach Bunn** (1971 Bluebook)

John continues: *One last memory of that year – by mistake, my name was "checked" in the scorebook as a starter for a varsity game. So when Mr. Cook, the PA announcer, announced me as a starter, I was shocked. Coach instructed me to not handle the ball – give it to John Oistad until he could get me out of the game. We ended up in third place in District 32 that year.*

**Coach Musburger presented Kennedy players Richard Murray (#13), Wayne Hultgren (#21) and Tom Lundgren their 2nd place district trophy after losing to Stephen in 1971.**
(11 March 1971, *Karlstad Advocate*)

The **1971 football** team, led by captains John Oistad and Jon Nordine, opened the season by defeating a very good Baudette squad 12-6. The team continued their season defeating Oslo, Kennedy, Greenbush, Argyle and Lancaster and losing to Drayton and Newfolden for a 6-2 record. Varsity players included Tim Vagle, Glen Spilde, Kent Hanson, Jon Nordine, John Oistad, David Peterson, Dean Johnson, John Erickson, Don Johnson, Gus Berggren, Orlin Anderson, Kent Benson, Roger Jacobson, James Anderson, Jim Musburger, Jerry Olson, David Vik, Tim Andersen, Ken Johnson, Dan Anderson, Greg Wierschke, Greg Dahlin, Rick Netterlund, student manager Tim Lutz and coaches Phil Johnson and Jim Musburger.

**Karlstad Varsity Football Team 1970-71: Row 1:  T. Vagle, G. Spilde, K. Hanson, J. Nordine, J. Oistad, D. Peterson.  Row 2:  Coach Musburger, T. Lutz, manager, D. Johnson, J. Erickson, D. Johnson, G. Berggren, O. Anderson, Coach Johnson.  Row 3:  K. Benson, R. Jacobson, J. Anderson, J. Musburger, J. Olson, D. Vik.  Fourth Row: T. Anderson, K. Johnson, D. Anderson, G. Wierschke, G. Dahlin, R. Netterlund.** (1971 Bluebook)

All conference selections were Glen Spilde, Jerry Olson, Kent Hanson and John Oistad.

**Jon Nordine '71**, captain of the football team, recalls:  *I did not serve in the military, but I perceived Coach Musburger as a drill sergeant.  His basketball coaching record speaks for itself.  As 10th, 11th or 12th man on the basketball team, I remember how excited I was to finally play with the big boys.  I can't forget running figure 8s with the medicine ball and trying to shoot the dumb thing.  My dad, newspaper editor Dane Nordine, thought a great deal of Jim Musburger.*

Varsity cheerleaders were Colleen Koland, Pamela Oistad, Monica Boen, Margo Dagen, Cynthia Vik and Diedre Pederson.

**1971 "K" Letterman's Club** (1971 Bluebook)

The main objective of the "K" Letterman's Club was a trip to the state basketball tournament at Williams Arena in Minneapolis, Minnesota.

**Kent Hanson** tells a funny story traveling to the tournament in 1970: *Our team traveled with Hallock and Kennedy players on a bus to share transportation costs and stayed at the Hampshire Arms Hotel in Minneapolis. We thought we were in an assisted living hotel as we were the youngest by 50 years. Oh yes, black and white TVs, old people in the dining rooms and they actually lived there. Chris Johnson was sticking his head out the window and making animal sounds when we got to the cities.*

# 16. KARLSTAD RABBITS 1971-72

*One random memory of mine involved the bus rides coming home from "away" games. We would often travel eastbound on highway 11. Inevitably, there was a "dip" in the road, as we got closer to Karlstad. Norman Berg would often be our driver and as we approached that dip, the bus chanted very loudly, "hit that bump, Norman—hit that bump!" Without slowing down, he would do just that. I recall being lifted out of my seat and would see Norman's raised fist at the wheel. Coach helped build this team spirit – even with a pretty serious guy like Norman.* – John Erickson '72

Despite losing four starters from the previous year, the 1972 basketball team ended their season 14-6. Varsity players included seniors John Erickson, Bob Johnson, Jim Musburger (Captain and All-Conference), Jerry Olson and Mark Sang; juniors Terry Anderson, David Grandstrand and Tim Johnson; sophomores Rick Netterlund and Kenny Johnson; freshmen David Vik, Lee Sele and student manager Matt Berg.

**Karlstad Rabbits Varsity Basketball Team 1971-72: Left to right: R. Netterlund, T. Anderson, K. Johnson, J. Olson, M. Sang, D. Vik, J. Musburger, D. Grandstrand, T. Johnson, J. Erickson, B. Johnson, L. Sele, M. Berg, manager.** (1972 Bluebook)

The Rabbits finished 2nd in the west sub-district conference and as a result, were seeded into the District 32 tournament without playing in the sub-district tournament. They placed 3rd in the district tournament by defeating Baudette 61-40, followed by a heartbreaking loss to the Newfolden Nordics 54-52. A Nordic ball heading out of bounds bounced off the referees foot, bounced back on the court, was picked up by a Nordic and put in the basket by Mike Sollum to tie the game. Then with three seconds remaining, Donovan Nelson scored the winning bucket for Newfolden.

The consolation game ended with a win over Kennedy 62-54. Jimmy Musburger led all scoring with 34 points followed by Jim Dahl from Kennedy with 19 points. (16 March 1972, page 4, North Star News)

Varsity cheerleaders were Debby Koland, Cindy Vik, Pam Oistad, Kim Carlson, Monica Boen and Marcia Spilde.

The desire to play for the Rabbits was a childhood dream for **John Erickson '72**. He reminisces about his journey to varsity play for Karlstad: *My first memories of Coach Musburger were watching him coach the Strandquist Warriors against the Karlstad coach, Wally Boen. I was really young, six or seven, but my recollections of both coaches were that they were both quite intense – almost scary. In a few years, however, I lost some of my fear of him when his son, Jimmy, and I became good friends – meaning I hung out at his home frequently and was able to see Jimmy's dad as a parent, who just happened to be a coach.*

*During 1965-1968, I fantasized of playing for Mr. Musburger's A team. The 1966 District 32 championship team was electrifying. I wanted to be like Neil Wikstrom, Neil Skogerboe, Tim Olson, Ernie Pietruszewski and Brian Sjodin. I felt that the non-starters, Troy Dagen, Tom Folland and Glenn Peterson, contributed greatly to the team's success. School spirit and community pride in KHS basketball was everywhere. Dean Dahlin, my 6th grade teacher, encouraged us to make posters during the tournament season, which would be hung throughout the school to show school support. I still remember having my contribution censored because it featured a shapely woman with my caption, "get your rear in gear & go the game." During those years, as well as from 1969-1972, the Rabbits finished no lower than 4th place in District 32 tournaments.*

*I made the team in 1970, the 12th player on a 12-man roster. It was a* great year. We won the District 32 championship. Anticipating a long run for that season, Coach scheduled games with three "big" schools: East Grand Forks, Thief River Falls and Bemidji. All of the games were played **at** their gymnasiums. We lost our game with EGF, but won both JV and Varsity games at TRF and Bemidji. After the Bemidji game, we needed to be escorted to our team bus due to the hostility of the local fans. What a great tribute to the small-town team! I remember that Coach had one ace up his sleeve for the post season. That was inserting his son, Jimmy, a sophomore, into the lineup. That move, along with having talented veterans like Lowell Sjodin, Jerry Pietruszewski. Chris Johnson, Jerry Kuznia., Kent Hanson, Richie Pietruszewski, Stuart Spilde, Harlan Bengtson, John Oistad, Glen Spilde and Jerry Olson, made this team very strong.

In 1972, my senior year, I got to live my dream and started on the KHS varsity team. Unlike 1971, he made me the primary ball handler. He trusted me—I felt that. He had us prepared and confident. Granted, without Jimmy's overall leadership, we would have been in trouble, but as a result of the previous two years of playing together, we were prepared and finished third place once again in District 32. We actually played a 1-3-1 zone defense that year. This was a deviation from our man-to man defensive history. Great fun. During my senior year just before the last game of the season, my dad died from an aneurysm. Basketball helped me compartmentalize and get through my grief.

Coach was a very intentional and strategic person. He had drills and clichés meant to build skills and good team attitude. I remember wearing those "horse blinder glasses" during our pivoting on the dribble drills. They made it impossible to look at the ball while dribbling – "keep your head up, boys." At the beginning of our seasons, he attached smaller diameter rims to the regular rims to make us shoot with a greater arch. It was a great day when they were removed!

Among life lessons learned and greatest blessings of playing for Coach Musburger included the self-confidence and self- discipline he taught and expected from me. To repeat, in 1970, he had the confidence in his team to schedule games with three much larger schools. We won two of the three games at their gyms. Very "Hoosiers-like." All of the experience and observations I've made as a result of knowing Coach

*Musburger helped me greatly in my work life. I'm now retired, but in my last position, I represented a smaller company than our major competitors. I truly was able to integrate the "no fear" attitude learned from Coach into my work. We won much more than we lost. So to Coach Musburger, "Thank you for believing in us. We were always prepared and fundamentally sound. It was a true privilege to have you in my life."*

**Myra Fleener:** You know, a basketball hero around here is treated like a god, er, uh, how can he ever find out what he can really do? I don't want this to be the high point of his life.

**Coach Norman Dale:** You know, most people would kill... to be treated like a god, just for a few moments.

*–"The Hoosiers"*

**1972 Seniors**
**John Erickson, Bob Johnson, Jim Musburger, Mark Sang, Jerry Olson** (1972 Bluebook)

Led by seniors Dean and Donovan Johnson (co-captains), Gus Berggren, Jerry Olson, Jim Musburger and John Erickson, the 1971-72 football team defeated Baudette, Hallock and Drayton, tied Kennedy, and lost to Argyle, Oslo, Greenbush and Newfolden for a 3-1-4 season record. Jerry Olson, Jim Musburger and Donovan Johnson won all-conference honors.

**Coach Musburger** recalls recruiting twin brothers Dean and Donovan Johnson for the football team: *Heck and I drove out to Lloyd Johnson's farm to ask if they would let Dean and Don go out for football. They eventually consented but not before Mrs. Johnson said, "If anything happens to their teeth, you will regret it!"*

**Karlstad Varsity Football Team 1971-72: Row 1: G. Berggren, D. Johnson, J. Olson, J. Musburger, J. Erickson, D. Johnson. Row 2: D. Linde, K. Johnson, K. Olson, S. Andersen, T. Nelson, T. Johnson, R. Netterlund. Row 3: Coach Johnson, D. Grahn, G. Wierschke, D. Anderson, G. Dahlin, R. Hanson, L. Sele, Coach Musburger, Row 4: D. Sele, R. Jacobson, J. Anderson, K. Benson, L. Cormeir, R. Haugen, T. Johnson, T. Lutz.** (1972 Bluebook)

**Football Seniors 1972:  Gus Berggren, Jerry Olson, Jim Musburger, John Erickson, Dean Johnson, Donovan Johnson** (1972 Bluebook)

**Kim Carlson '74** (1972 Bluebook)

# 17. KARLSTAD RABBITS 1972-73

*During the Stephen game, I had a terrible sore throat and could hardly breathe, so Coach personally took an ordinary white towel, soaked it in Icy Hot, wrapped it around my neck, taped it in place and sent me out there. I played the whole game with that towel around my neck, but the fans, and my parents among them, could not understand why the coach was playing me with a neck brace.* – David Grandstrand '73

**Karlstad Varsity Basketball Team 1972-73: Front row: Dan Sele, Ken Johnson, Terry Anderson, Lee Sele, Ricky Netterlund. Back row: Dave Vik, David Grandstrand, Tim Johnson, Wayne Altendorf, Dan Sandahl, Denal Grahn, Rick Olson.** (1973 Bluebook)

In 1972 -1973, the Varsity basketball team, led by Seniors David Grandstrand (all-conference), Terry Anderson and Tim Johnson (captain and all-conference) were coached by Musburger and Bunn with student managers Doug Sele, Keith Olson and Matt Berg taking care of all the details. The Rabbits struggled in 1973, losing close games to Roseau, Mentor, and Newfolden. Highlights of the year were victories over Argyle 55-52, Lancaster 54-51 and Middle River 63-62 to end the season with an 8-12 record. The Rabbits defeated Hallock 73-58 in the District tournament before falling to Kennedy 58-53 and Middle River 59-49.

Varsity cheerleaders were Marcia Spilde, Barbara Locken, Cindy Vik, Kim Carlson, Kristi Anderson and DeEtte Stamnes.

**David Grandstrand '73** recalls playing Rabbit basketball: *One thing Musburger did for the team, that was especially valuable to me, was to provide drivers to take players home after practice. Without that, there is no way I would have been able to participate in the basketball program. Loren Germundson and Tilden Spilde from Halma were a couple of the regulars that drove me halfway to Stephen every night. Another clear memory is from my freshman year, which was my first year at Karlstad. JV and varsity practiced together and there was no doubt in anyone's mind that I was the worst player on the floor that year. Every practice we would do some layups and, often times, we would do layups until we went through a full rotation of the team without missing one. I know that Kent, Lowell, Jim, Chris and the others did a lot more layups because of me that year; but everyone, including Musburger, gave me the chance to improve.*

*One particular game memory from my senior year was playing Stephen at Stephen. It was a particularly meaningful game for me as I had attended Stephen through 8th grade so I knew all their players quite well. One of those players was Greg Kuznia, who was at least 5 inches taller than I was. I won the opening tip off, but he made things difficult for me for the remainder of the game. The game was also memorable as Musburger did one of his usual patch jobs to get his players on the court. I had a terrible sore throat and could hardly breathe, so he personally took an ordinary white towel, soaked it in Icy Hot (or whatever similar product we used at the time), wrapped it around my neck, taped it in place and sent me out there. I played the whole game with that towel around my neck but the fans, and my parents among them, could not understand why the coach was playing me with a neck brace.*

*One other lasting memory was the senior banquet when Musburger would say nice things about his departing seniors. He started my introduction with "this is the kid that couldn't walk and chew gum at the same time" and I remember thinking, "that's an 'interesting' way to introduce your all-conference center. Finally, a memory outside of basketball - playing dodge ball in phy-ed. I don't recall there being any rules, so coming out of phy-ed with a welt was more the rule than the exception. And still we pleaded with Musburger to let us play more dodge ball.*

*My #1 takeaway from those four years is a bit of philosophy that continues to guide me even now decades later. I can still hear Musburger saying, "Expect the best...prepare for the worst," on multiple occasions my senior year. That statement has been the guiding principle behind all the "what if" questions I have asked during my career as a banker.*

**David Grandstrand, Coach Musburger, Tim Johnson**
(1973 Bluebook)

**Kenny Johnson #23, David Vik #43, playing against Strandquist**
(1973 Bluebook)

**Coach Phil Johnson** weighs in on the 1972-73 football team: *Our record was 4-4-1 that year. Captains were Roger Jacobson and Kent Benson. Roger, Kent, Tim Andersen and Rick Netterlund were all-conference . We did not have lights, so we still played afternoon games, our last year without lights. The season started well with non-conference victories but an injury to a key player caused the team to miss out on some late season opportunities.*

Karlstad Varsity Football Team 1972-73:
Row 1: Greg Dahlin, Don Anderson, Ken Johnson, Ricky Netterlund, Matt Berg, Roger Jacobson, Kent Benson, Robert Hanson, Tim Andersen, Bob Haugen, Terry Pearson. Row 2: Coach Phil Johnson, Ted Johnson, Lee Sele, Denal Grahn, Adrian Cormier, Todd Carlson, Wayne Lutz, Dan Sele, Luther Germundson, David Vik, Coach Jim Musburger. Row 3: Tim Lutz, Doug Sele, James Anderson, Daniel Sandahl, Ricky Olson, Dan Clark, Jim Nordine, Ron Slaathaug, John Downhour.
(1973 Bluebook)

Homecoming 1973 (1973 Bluebook)

**Homecoming 1973:  Head football coach Phil Johnson,
Assistant Coach Jim Musburger** (1973 Bluebook)

# 18. KARLSTAD RABBITS 1973-74

*There is one game and tournament run that I will always remember. My senior year we won three very close games before losing to Argyle in the district finals at Roseau. Our game against our biggest rival Kennedy was truly a highlight. I can remember getting down by 18 points and thinking this is it. At a time out, Coach said we are switching to a zone defense. He gave us our marching orders and to hustle until we get back into this game. We pulled that game out in the last seconds to go to the district finals.* – Ken Johnson '74

Led by seniors Rick "Netty" Netterlund (captain), Wayne "Alty" Altendorf, and Ken Johnson (captain), the 1973-1974 varsity basketball team included juniors Denal Grahn, Dan Sandahl, Lee Sele, and David Vik; sophomores Dan Clark, Luther Germundson, Randy Hultgren, Todd Carlson, Mike Kuznia, Steve Lofstrom, Jim Nordine and Dan Sele; and freshman Loel Olson. Jim Musburger and George Bunn coached the team and managers Keith Olson, Doug Sele and Terry Pearson kept the team in order. All-conference selections were David Vik and Ken Johnson. David Vik was also elected to the Prep All-American team.

Karlstad Varsity Basketball Team 1973-74: Front row: Coach Bunn, R. Netterlund, L. Olson, D. Sele, K. Johnson, R. Olson, L. Sele, Coach Musburger. Back row: D. Sele, D. Sandahl, M. Kuznia, D. Vik, K. Olson, L. Germundson, W. Altendorf, D. Grahn, T. Pearson.

This talented team won the sub-district tournament by defeating Hallock 73-57 and tipped Stephen in overtime, 61-59, on a last-second shot by Mike Kuznia to claim the title. At District play in Newfolden, the Rabbits won two nail biters by defeating Roseau 62-61 and Kennedy 45-44 before losing the championship game to Argyle 60-50. During the Roseau game, the Ram's Ross Thacker nailed two free throws to tie the game at 60 followed by Carl Fugleberg's free throw to put Roseau ahead 61-60. Karlstad took the ball out of bounds, the pass went to Lee Sele at midcourt and then to David Vik for the winning layup. The Kennedy game was equally exciting. At the end of the game, Ken Johnson stole the ball and made a layup to win the game. This was the year of three buzzer-beater and overtime thrillers (Stephen, Roseau, Kennedy) that took the 1974 team to the District finals.

**Coach Musburger** vividly remembers the win over Kennedy: *We lost to Kennedy twice that season by 20 points each time and really had no business playing in the district finals. Glen Spilde, Sr. threatened to quit attending basketball games, as he was afraid he would have a heart attack. Kenny Johnson stole the ball, made a lay-up and the game ended and we won – big upset. After the game, Louis Deere said to me, "You never got a foul called on you." I replied, "Louis, you know we always play a clean game."*

**Loel Olson '77** recalls tournament play: *Down by two, seconds left against Stephen, in Hallock, 1974 sub-district championship. I'm on the bench as a freshman. Sophomore Mike Kuznia gets the ball twenty feet out on the right offensive baseline. He brings the ball up to shoot, and I swear it slipped out of his hands on the way up. Ball in the air, buzzer goes off, and it swishes through the net to tie up the game. Mike's quoted in the paper, saying, "I just threw it up!" Phil Johnson, the football coach, later said that Mike, who was very, very good, was also the luckiest athlete he had ever seen. It still makes me laugh.*

*The Rabbits won two games by one point each in overtime, which started the greatest run I ever saw in sports. In front of "please squeeze to the middle of the gymnasium" crowds, Karlstad beat Roseau 62-61 in the District quarterfinals when David Vik scored on a fast break lay-up with three seconds left. Senior Kenny Johnson stole the ball at mid court and made his normal smooth left handed lay-up to upset the extremely good Kennedy Rockets 45-44 in the semifinals. For three games I was the happiest bench player on the planet. Ken, Dave Vik, Ricky Netterlund, Luther Germundson, Mike Kuznia, Danny and Lee Sele... it was simply magic.*

*It ended against Argyle in the District championship a couple of nights later where Richard Sletten ate me alive and we ended up losing in a jam-packed Newfolden gym. We are the # 2 seed from the west side, and have been ahead of #1 seed Argyle the whole game, beating their press often and playing great defense. The lead fades in the 4th quarter, and with 15 seconds left, Argyle scores, tying the game at 55. I take the ball out of bounds, the noise is deafening, and the only guy I can find to pass to is Lee Sele heading down court. I try to loft it over Argyle's Ken Safranski, who leaps twelve feet in the air to snag it. He comes in for a lay-up, he scores, I'm called for a foul, he makes the free throw, and we lose 58-57.*

**Starters: Rick Netterlund, Dan Sele, Lee Sele, Mike Kuznia, Dave Vik, Ken Johnson** (1974 Bluebook)

**Ken Johnson '74** recalls the team of '74: *Being a part of the school and the sports scene in the 70's at Karlstad High School was very special. The coaches, fans, businesses and school staff all supported us at a high level. We had great rivalries with the schools in the area. Going up against Kennedy led by Coach Deere and Argyle led by Coach Keller were always great games. I am really grateful to have been a student and athlete under Mr. Musburger's leadership. In the classroom Mr. Musburger had our respect and our attention, but he always made it fun for his students. Some of Coach Musburger's style has been with me throughout my life.*

*In the 70's short hair was not the "in" thing unless you were a Karlstad Rabbit basketball player. After football season he let us know to get our hair cut prior to the first practice. You had a standing appointment every week or two with Jay the barber in Karlstad! Having polished football spikes and white converse shoes was also rare unless you played for Karlstad High School. Our team always looked very nice wearing the dark blue blazers with a tie to our basketball games. I will never forget Coach George Bunn teaching us how to tie our neck ties. He said we don't need to wear clip-ons, so he taught us how to properly wear a neck tie, a great life skill. I didn't realize it at the time, but Mr. Musburger was teaching us that you only get one chance to make your first impression. He also knew that if his teams were making good first impressions, they would be better at the task at hand, whether it was how he prepared us for the game, discipline, passion to improve, or how we looked and presented ourselves on and off the court. I vividly remember the many compliments our teams received for our haircuts and our team appearance from opposing coaches and game officials.*

*I do need to mention how special it was for the basketball team to have "fridge rights" at the school. The cooks at Karlstad loved making us no-bake cookies and apple crisp. After some practices we'd eat and drink milk and laugh to no end. What a great memory. Coach helped us build great team memories with our classmates as well as the younger and older team members.*

*There is one game and tournament run that I will always remember. My senior year we won three very close games before losing to Argyle in the district finals. Our game against our biggest rival*

*Kennedy was truly a highlight. I can remember getting down by 18 points and thinking this is it. At a time out Coach said we are switching to a zone defense. He gave us our marching orders and to hustle until we get back into this game. Losing to Coach Deere's teams was never fun. Before long we were catching up and with a couple of minutes left in the game we were within reach. We pulled that game out in the last seconds to go to the district finals. We trusted our Coaches, the zone defense worked. They had faith in our team.*

**Loel Olson** admired his team captain: *As a freshman, I found myself looking up to senior Ken Johnson. Kenny was not a star, but was a fun, articulate, charismatic leader who played his best basketball down a tournament stretch that I can never forget. He also led on us on a few after practice pie-snatching escapades to the home-ec room. For whatever reason, practice would end, the coaches would leave, and Kenny would take over to lead us on one of his famous raids. I can still remember him with a slice of pie in his hand and a big grin on his face. Today that type of thing would probably get us suspended, but at the time it was huge fun.*

**Coach George Bunn, Coach Jim Musburger, Danny Clark, Danny Sele and Lee Sele** (1974 Bluebook)

**Larry Peterson, Roseau Rams coach**, recalls coaching against the Rabbits in 1974: *I got my first boys basketball coaching position in Roseau, Minnesota, from 1974-79. I was lucky to be coaching against some basketball legends in Minnesota. At the time, Jim Musburger was the dean of those coaches. His teams were always well coached, well disciplined, fundamentally sound, excellent defensively and always tough to beat. Needless to say even though we had some good teams at Roseau during this time, we were 1 and 4 vs. Karlstad. I learned a lot from Jim and the other great coaches in northwest Minnesota at this time. Jim was a class act whether winning or losing. No matter what the situation, he always seemed to have a plan to exploit the weakness of his opponent. He was a credit to the coaching profession and was a winner and mentor for me.*

**Team manager Keith Olson '74** offers his perspective: *I respected Coach Musburger and the basketball program in Karlstad. I wanted to be part of the team and that whole experience, even though my basketball skills were not at the level that included me as a player. When I was asked to take on the role as manager, I was part of the Karlstad Rabbits basketball program and all the fun and excitement. I could be with my friends and provide a service to the team.*

*Forty-five plus years later, specific details don't come readily to me. However, one specific event does come to mind. I would prepare the stats book with names of the team members, share it with the opposing team and then receive their names. One game, I inadvertently left out a player on the roster. The game started and I was at the table entering the shots, fouls and scores. The person from the other team with his book sat next to me. Sometime into that game, Coach sent in that one player. The other scorekeeper noticed that this player was not in the book and immediately asked for the buzzer. My mistake was discovered, the buzzer rang, the game stopped, and I received a technical foul. Everyone was asking who had the technical. Soon everyone in the gymnasium knew what I had done. I was quite embarrassed. Coach was very gracious and kind to me when I easily could have gotten a "chewing out."*

Led by senior Co-captains Ken Johnson and Rick Netterlund, and seniors Robert Haugen, Danny Anderson, Terry Pearson, Robert Hanson, Tim Andersen and Greg Dahlin, the 1974 football team placed third in conference play with a 5-4 season record. Other varsity athletes included Ron Austad, Daniel Smith, Brian Sele, Ron Slaathaug, Neil Germundson, Lee Sele, Rick Olson, Wayne Lutz, Denal Grahn, Darwyn Anderson, Dan Sele, Greg Dahlin, Dan Sandahl, David Vik, Teddy Johnson, managers Rod Brown, Byron Bengtson and Tim Lutz, and coaches Phil Johnson and Jim Musburger. All-conference selections were Rick Netterlund, Tim Andersen, Ken Johnson and Greg Dahlin.

**Karlstad Varsity Football Team 1973-74: Front row: R. Austad, R. Netterlund, T. Andersen, D. Smith, B. Sele. Second row: Coach Johnson, R. Slaathaug, N. Germundson, L. Sele, R. Hanson, R. Olson, W. Lutz, Coach Musburger. Third row: D. Grahn, D. Anderson, K. Johnson, D. Sele, G. Dahlin, T. Pearson. Fourth row: B. Bengtson, manager, R. Haugen, D. Sandahl, T. Lutz, manager, D. Vik, T. Johnson, R. Brown, manager.** (1974 Bluebook)

**Varsity Cheerleaders: Barbara Johnson, Kristi Anderson, DeEtte
Stamnes, Barbara Locken, Holly Grandstrand, Kim Carlson**

**B Team Cheerleaders: Suzanne Johnson, Ann Germundson,
Carolyn Wikstrom, Tracy Pederson, Polly Anderson**
(1974 Bluebook)

# 19. KARLSTAD RABBITS 1974-75

*Coach loved effort, smarts and fundamentals over talent any day.*
*He believed that the "harder you work, the luckier you got."* --
Danny Clark '76

The 1975 Basketball Varsity team narrowly missed a bid to the
regional tournament by defeating Roseau 57-38 and Greenbush 56-54
before losing a thriller to Argyle 58-57 at the District tournament in
Newfolden. The talented roster included seniors Denal Grahn, Dan
Sandahl, and Lee Sele (captain); juniors Danny Clark, Luther
Germundson, Randy Hultgren, Mike Kuznia (All- Conference), Steve
Lofstrom, Jim Nordine, Rick Olson, Dan Sele, Todd Carlson;
sophomores Loel Olson and Neil Germundson; freshmen Brian
Bothum and Tim Porter; managers Jody Pearson and Doug Sele; and
coaches Jim Musburger and George Bunn. Giving a nod to equal
opportunity for girls in sports, Jody Pearson signed on as the first
female team manager. They also took home the Thief River Falls
Tournament championship by defeating Thief River Falls and Fosston.

**Karlstad Rabbits Varsity Basketball Team 1974-75:**
**Front row: Student manager J. Pearson, L. Sele, S. Lofstrom, D.**
**Clark, D. Sele, R. Olson, J. Nordine, Student manager D. Sele. Back**
**row: Coach Musburger, R. Hultgren, T. Porter, N. Germundson, D.**
**Sandahl, L. Germundson, M. Kuznia, B. Bothum, D. Grahn, L.**
**Olson, Coach Bunn.** (1975 Bluebook)

Varsity cheerleaders were Barb Johnson, Kris Anderson, Charlene Helling, Carla Oistad, Carol Vik and Holly Grandstrand.

**Lee Sele '75** recalls losing the district in 1975: *The loss to Argyle was a heartbreaker as we lost in the last 30 seconds. We were up by one with 31 seconds to go and the ball out of bounds under their basket. Ken Safranski stole the inbound pass, made a layup and was fouled for a 3- point play to win that game. Worst minute of my time on Jim's teams!*

Assistant Argyle Coach **John Schmidt** remembers the Argyle win: *We were in the huddle and I told Ken Safranski what to do if he missed the basket. Ken said to me, "I won't miss, I will make it." Ken scored two baskets and a free throw, five points, to win the game in the last seconds. Jim cried at the end of the game.* **Coach Musburger** never forgot the loss to Argyle or the win against Greenbush the night before: *The Greenbush fans sat right behind our bench and after we won the game, I jumped up and a Greenbush woman pulled me down by my suit coat. Argyle ended up beating us for the championship.*

**Danny Clark '76** tells about basketball that year: *I vividly remember how every year after football season and in the first two weeks of basketball conditioning, Coach would promise me that I would need suspenders for my trunks in a couple of weeks. He loved effort, smarts and fundamentals over talent any day. He believed that the "harder you work, the luckier you got." He also believed in man-to man- defense and when it came to zone defense, he stepped aside and let Coach Bunn take over. He did not like using zone but knew it was a necessary evil that we had to master. Coach was strict, stern and cared deeply how we turned out as men as much as he cared how good we were in basketball.*

**Lee Sele** wrote about a game with Drayton: *He always gave me such a tough time about my flutter when I shot a jump shot. He often said he knew it was going in when he saw that flutter. I remember a game against Drayton my junior year. They were tall and playing a 1-2-2 zone so we needed to shoot from the perimeter. I was on the bench for a breather and he turned and looked at me and asked how I was feeling and I told him I'm great and was shooting well that night. He smiled and said, "What the hell are you doing on the bench then? Get in there!" I spent many study halls my last two years of school down in the* *gym shooting free throws when we were supposed to be washing towels and uniforms. He would never admit it to anyone but I'm pretty sure he knew. I always had such respect for him as he treated everyone in the whole program the same whether a starter or a student manager.*

**Loel Olson'77** comments: *Perhaps most interesting about that basketball team was that the best player in the conference that year never played. Senior David Vik had scored 342 points as a junior, was all-conference, and simply an atypical physical specimen for that area. He's listed as 6'0" in the District program from 1974, and if he was 6 feet tall, I was Mighty Mouse. He was easily 6'2", maybe 6'3", weighed somewhere in the 235-pound range, and was simply a smooth, gifted athlete. He was also a fun guy, a great teammate, and always the one you wanted on your team in grade school, from King of the Hill to the spring baseball games. After a great senior football season, he was in an awkward situation, having married a second cousin of mine and expecting a child. He never did go out for basketball, and projecting what might have been for Karlstad is impossible.*

Led by seniors Lee Sele (co-captain) Denal Grahn, Teddy Johnson and David Vik (co-captain), the 1974-75 football team ended the season with a winning 7-2 record. Underclassman included Ron Slaathaug, Danny Clark, Wayne Lutz, Ron Austad, Brian Sele, Jim Cardinal, John Downhour, Danny Sele, Mike Kuznia, Luther Germundson, Todd Carlson, Rick Olson, Tim Lutz, manager and coaches Phil Johnson and Jim Musburger. Lee Sele and David Vik were All- Conference.

## 20.  KARLSTAD RABBITS 1975-76

*Coach had a key to the school kitchen and the players would eat all the dessert after practice.  The next morning, the intercom would announce, "Because of the high school basketball team, there will be no dessert for lunch."* – Randy Hultgren '76

The 1976 Karlstad Rabbits were a force to behold in conference and district play.  This talented and exciting team won the conference title and went on to win the District 32 tournament by defeating Roseau 58-47, Middle River 63-53, and Baudette 39-38 to advance to the regional tournament in Grand Forks.  Coach Musburger stated that Randy and Luther had their best games ever against Middle River.  The Rabbits lost to Mahnomen 59-42 in the first round and then defeated Northome 54-52 for third place.  Mahnomen won the region tournament and advanced to the state tournament.

Karlstad Varsity Basketball Team 1975-76:  Row 1:  B. Nelson, L. Olson, L. Swanson.  Row 2:  D. Sele, R. Hultgren, L. Germundson, M. Kuznia, D. Clark, T. Carlson.  Row3:  Coach Musburger, D. Anderson, S. Rowland, B. Bothum, N. Germundson, T. Porter, W. Lutz, Coach Bunn .(1976 Bluebook)

Led by co-captains Mike Kuznia and Danny Sele, the roster included Brad Nelson, Loel Olson, Lowell Swanson, Randy Hultgren, Luther

Germundson, Danny Clark, Todd Carlson, Darwyn Anderson, Steve Rowland, Brian Bothum, Neil Germundson, Tim Porter, Wayne Lutz, manager Scott Thompson and scorer Jody Pearson. All-Conference players were Mike Kuznia and Loel Olson.

**Randy Hultgren '76** tells about the athlete's desire to excel: *I wasn't that good in football but they needed players so I went out for the team. We played Esko and took 2<sup>nd</sup> in state in football, coached by Phil Johnson and Jim Musburger. Danny Clark was the best football player and later coached football in Karlstad and basketball in Strandquist. We also went to regionals in basketball and started five seniors: Luther Germundson, Danny Clark (6<sup>th</sup> man), Danny Sele, Mike Kuznia and Randy Hultgren. Loel Olson, a junior, started on the varsity. We were very mature seniors and could really shoot, all five of us. We had played together since 4<sup>th</sup> grade. Coach said that Danny Sele was the best point guard, best defensive player he ever had on a team. Danny started for three years on the varsity. As a kid, I would stand on a snow bank on the farm and shoot baskets for hours.*

*We were driven, passionate and talented. Five other seniors quit as they knew they would not get to play – we had so much talent and depth. Some seniors were upset that Loel, a junior, was a starter, but Loel was our best player. We worked hard in practice and the best free throw shooter, Mike Kuznia, won a plaque. We were all in superb shape and I remember never feeling winded.*

*I broke my collar bone my junior year and started my senior year. We had a tough conference – Baudette and Middle River were really good. We won conference and had two All-Conference players. We beat Baudette for the district championship. Danny Clark got into their center, Mike Carrier's head, and Mike lost his temper and kept getting called for charging. He ended up fouling out and I feel like Danny, who was a solid brick, won the game for us. I played my best game and my whole family watched me play that night.*

*Every year we wore $10 white Converse tennis shoes for our game shoes. Well, our senior year, Converse came out with a navy suede low cut shoe, and we really wanted those cool shoes. We talked the coach into it but the price was $18, a lot of money in 1976. I remember my mom scolding*

142

the coach that the shoes were an extra $8! Also that year, Coach relented and let us grow our hair a little below our ears. Looking back on the pictures, we look terrible with our hair swept down over the tops of our glasses and ears. Of course, we thought we looked good at the time and our girlfriends approved. If you played on varsity, you were guaranteed a girlfriend. Coach scheduled some games on Saturday night, like Bemidji or Baudette, and we had midnight curfew. I know he did this to keep us out of trouble.

I recall some funny stories. Coach had a key to the school kitchen and the players would eat all the dessert. The next morning, the intercom would announce, "Because of the high school basketball team, there will be no dessert for lunch." So the janitors changed the lock to the kitchen door, but we figured out how to get into the kitchen through the ceiling.

The coach ruled from haircuts to cars. Jay Spilde, the local barber, cut all our hair. We tried to get Jay to cut our hair a little longer, but he knew how coach wanted our hair and refused. One game Mike Kuznia was not playing well, he had a bad game. Coach called time out and chewed Mike out and told him to drive his car in the lake. No strategy at all, but we did not question anything coach said. And Superintendent Helling stood behind our coach, he had coach's back. During another game in Kennedy, a fight broke out on the floor with eight minutes left. One of the players punched me in the kidney and it really hurt. I flew at him with my fists, but Bunn grabbed me and pulled me off the floor. Well, I missed the first free throw and that guy stood there and clapped. I looked at him, smiled and pointed at the scoreboard. We were ahead with a few seconds left and won the game. And Argyle was tough - they were small and mean Frenchmen. When I played on the B team at their stage gym, we beat them in double overtime. We were so excited and pumped up, that the A team fired up and won their game, too.

During our senior year, fans in the community would buy the team, coaches and managers, about 20 of us, dinner at Hanson's Café twice a week. We always had the same meal: Swiss steak, mashed potatoes and corn. After several weeks of the same meal, Coach looked at his plate, and said, "Can you imagine that? Swiss steak." I just cracked up and I still laugh every time I think about it. I remember Tilden and Shirley Spilde had us out to their home for barbecues every year. When we won *the district, crates of Gatorade and pop would show up at practice courtesy of the fans. The gym was packed for every game, and the announcer would ask fans to push together to make room for more people. I lived for basketball. I felt the pressure but fed off the crowd. The players had disagreements, which would involve a fight in the locker room with a disgruntled player who wasn't getting playing time, but coach did not interfere, and we would work it out. Coach had an uncanny way of letting problems work out on their own, and the players who weren't playing much would quit. He knew that we all had different personalities and responded differently to direction.*

*We played Baudette to win the district in 1976. They played zone and we played man-to-man defense but we beat them 39-38. Danny Clark had the ball with a few seconds left, hung onto it until the buzzer went off, and then he threw the ball straight up in the air. I will never forget it. Four teams went to region: Warren, Northome, Mahnomen and us. We played Mahnomen our first game and lost – they won the region and went to state. We beat Northome the next night.*

*You know I was scared as a 9th grader, scared of coach, but by my senior year, I would run through a brick wall for him. He had my back. George Bunn was harder on me. He always told me that I was better than I thought I was. Coach Musburger was like a second dad to me.*

**Coach Musburger** commented: *The Lancaster coach had an ax to grind and would not vote for Randy and Danny Sele who should have been all conference in 1976. The 2nd and 3rd place teams had three all-conference players and we had two. I was really mad about it. And I do remember telling Mike to get rid of his car.*

*The boys were hungry after long and strenuous practices. Superintendent Helling called me into his office, "Kids seem to be getting into the kitchen." I responded, "I don't know anything about it." Helling replied, "I bet you don't."*

144

*Randy Hultgren had a great tournament for the Karlstad Rabbits last week. His shooting from the outside was outstanding, but he also played well on the floor. He missed this rebound, however, as it was garnered by Bear (23) Brian Palm. #42 is Rabbit Mike Kuznia.* (11 March 1976, *North Star News*)

Randy tells the story that on one bus trip, assistant basketball coach George Bunn saw a moose running in the woods and said, *"That looks like Danny Sele."* The name stuck. **Danny "Moose" Sele '76** recalls changing schools: *I started playing basketball in 4th grade in Lake Bronson and continued in Karlstad when we consolidated schools the next year. My sophomore year, I moved up to varsity for the next three years. Our practices were really hard but a lot of fun. Coach would have former players come in to scrimmage against us and he always made me guard Chris Johnson '70, who had endless energy and could run all night.*

*I recall the district semifinals against Kennedy my sophomore year. Kennedy, with a veteran team, had beat us three times that year – two times during the regular season and then again at sub-district. But that*

145

*night, we tied the game at half, and were down by one point with seconds to go when Kenny Johnson stole the ball and scored to win the game. That is my favorite game, upsetting Kennedy in districts. Coach Musburger gave us confidence and had the ability to get the best out of people. His teams ALWAYS played up to their potential or more. He taught us to play together as a team, stressed fundamentals and to always take good shots.*

*We learned not to go into Hanson's Café if we played a bad game the night before. All the local guys would be there and they would give us a hard time. "What were you guys thinking? You should have done this." And on and on.*

*Another highlight of my senior year was defeating Fosston and Hendrum in the Thief River Falls Christmas tournament. We crushed Hendrum by 20 points. Our senior year, 1976, we played the district championship game against Baudette. We started out playing man-to-man defense but switched to zone as is was harder for Baudette's much bigger guys to break the zone. Coach Musburger's decision to switch our defense tactic won us the championship.*

*We respected everything Coach Musburger said and did. He kept politics out of player selection for his teams. He was not influenced by status or money, but only played the best players. The whole town came out for the games – the gym was packed with fans and standing room only. Our parents were so proud as well as the fans. Ted Hanson at Hanson's Café treated us to dinners as well as Tilden Spilde and Loren Germundson.*

*Our starting five still gets together except for Luther Germundson who died. We miss him. I have been a carpenter for 37 years and credit my coach with instilling that strong work ethic in me. You know, I go to games in the cities where I live, and they do not have the community pride and support that we experienced in our small town.*

146

Patiently waiting the presentation of the District Basketball Championship trophy are these Karlstad Rabbits. They appear pretty calm and collected considering they had just won a one-point decision over the Baudette Bears 39-38. But patience and basic calmness were probably some of the most important qualities displayed by this group as they won their laurels through three tough ball games. Note the net wrapped around Danny Sele's head – evidence that they did show some emotion at the conclusion of the game. (11 March 1976, *North Star News*)

**1976 co-captains Mike Kuznia and Dan Sele** (1976 Bluebook)

**Mike Kuznia'76** shares another side to Coach Musburger: *Coach was my driver's training instructor. He picked me up in the summer of 1973 at our farm, eight miles south of Karlstad and said, "Let's drive to Warren," because I told him that Warren is where I would probably take my driver's test. He fell asleep on the way to Warren AND on the way back to our farm! Guess he must have trusted my driving. Another story is that when I was a junior and we played at Hallock, I made a last-second shot that actually slipped out of my hands and almost hit the roof, but went in! All the players were cheering in amazement that we tied the score, and Coach told us sternly to quit celebrating because we hadn't won the game yet. We did win later. He also coached my brother, Jerry '70, who accidently drowned in Lake Bronson on the 4th of July 1975. Before Jerry died, coach would tease me, "don't be like your brother Jerry." He joked about having to put footprints on the floor for him. Coach was someone I respected, and he coached us young kids to play very hard and aggressive. I think I was the last player in Karlstad (when he coached) that got a 14-carat gold small basketball for being the best free throw shooter in a given season during A games. I won it in 1975, but in 1976 I just received a plaque. Coach said gold was getting too expensive, so Karlstad school quit the gold basketballs. Yes, I still have the gold basketball with KHS gold protruding letters and my free throw percentage engraved in it. I am very proud of it.*

 **Coach Musburger** remarked, *"We had no business winning the district in 1976. Once again, I had the hardest working athletes who beat better teams on sheer determination. When the Baudette coach complained bitterly about their loss to us, Dane Nordine let him have it in the newspaper.*

**Loel Olson** recounts the tournament: *1976, our junior year, was great with four of five starters returning, and Randy Hultgren taking the fifth spot. Danny Clark and Todd Carlson came off the bench. We were very experienced, and Luther and Mike made us reasonably tall. We won the conference to set up a #1 District seed. With that seed we couldn't play in the Sub-District, so we had several days without games going into the District.*

The District tournament provided no wild upsets as we beat Roseau and Middle River to get to the championship. Scary for us, however, was that Mike Kuznia hurt his foot before the tournament and never fully recovered the rest of the season. Danny Sele, Randy Hultgren, and I never took a break the whole tournament. In the championship game, Baudette was much taller than us and it was a tough game, but we won 39-38. The Baudette coach was quoted in the paper that he thought they were a better team than we were, which drew a few comments locally. By winning the District 32 title, we gave Mr. Musburger his 3rd title in 11 or 12 years, more than any other school during his District 32 tenure up to that point.

Randy Hultgren really got his long outside shot game working towards the end of the season; in five tournament games he scored 11, 20, 12, 10 and 6 points. It seems like every shot he made was from somewhere near the Arctic Circle. Winning the region without a healthy Mike Kuznia wasn't gonna happen, and I'm not sure that even if we were fully healthy we could have handled Mahnomen. Mike was taped to the hilt and had a lot of trouble moving. We lost to Mahnomen in the opening round 59-42. Warren, who we frequently scrimmaged, beat Northome. In the championship, Mahnomen's Paul Muckenhirn scored 18 points to beat Warren. He was a beast who was a University of North Dakota tight end in college. We still managed a 3rd place finish when we beat Northome. Kuznia scored 20 that game playing on one leg, which shows the depth of his talent. What I mostly remember is that we kept telling the normally selfless Danny Sele to shoot for once, for God's sake, since it was his last game, and he scored 12 from the top of the key.

Randy Hultgren's years of practice paid off in an unforgettable, deadly outside shot his senior year that carried us far. Danny Sele was the toughest defender and the most selfless offensive player I ever played with. And Mike Kuznia was amazing for three varsity years; tough on defense, a great rebounder, and a guy who could literally score at will.

**Luther Germundson lets fly with 2 points against the Baudette Bears. Karlstad won the championship 39-38.**
(11 March 1976, *North Star News*)

The coaching staff suffered a tough loss in 1976 when George Bunn, Musburger's assistant basketball coach for seven years, resigned and moved back to North Dakota. Bunn and Musburger held great respect for one another and worked well as a team. **George Bunn** weighs in on his years coaching with Jim Musburger: *I remember winning the district at Stephen and Lowell getting hurt; the UND trainer wrapped him for the regional but he still wasn't himself. We lost the region, gone on a bad sideline blocking call. Jim will remember what I said to the referee. That year our second five was the third best team in the district, and when Jimmy started on varsity, we had an all-conference player on the bench. Speaking of Jimmy – when he insisted on shooting too many 3-pointers, Jim would say, "Talk to him, George." He would shut the coach's room door and I would. I begged Jim to start him and when he did at the district, Jimmy was great. Jim knew what he was doing. The other coaches weren't ready for him. I think he had 15 out of 16 at free throw line.*

*That year we beat Bemidji, Thief River and East Grand Forks during the season. Jim was especially proud to beat Bemidji. On the way back from*
150

the game, we stopped to eat and the game was on the radio on a delayed broadcast. Jerry Pete broke everyone up as he called everything on the game ahead of the announcer. He remembered every play I think.

Jim will remember the game where we were behind with seconds to go and the other team had the ball. Jim said in the huddle we need the ball. Chris Johnson threw himself under the ball, picked it up and we scored. (Talk about going through a wall for your coach) Jim was the best man-to-man defensive coach I've ever worked with and he hated zones. But when my B team did well with our 1-2-1+1 zones press, he had me work on it with his team. We used it with success.

When Addy had hip surgery, I coached the team for several games including our win over Fosston. Jim went to the school board and insisted I get paid (respect). One of my proudest moments was reading the Minneapolis paper where Warren Keller, the Argyle coach, said he and his assistants copied Musburger and Bunn for coaching. Jim sent me the article.

Jim would come over most days and watch Jeopardy with me. He was great! He even knew opera. If ever I am on a quiz show, I want Jim as my lifeline. His knowledge of basketball is also Jeopardy quality.

Jim's practices were something – well run and disciplined. He believed in having a basketball in your hands at all times. I used 75% of his drills for 12 years after I left Karlstad. Phil Johnson was at one of my practices and said it was like being at Jim's practice. Jim was so open-minded with me. One year we had to cut players and one of the player's name came up. I argued that he was so smart and he would improve. Jim listened to me, and the player stayed. Most head coaches would never have listened to the assistant.

I have so many more memories. I could write a book, maybe a book about great coaches in the area would work: Louis Deere, Warren Keller, Jim Musburger, Jerry Snyder and Ron Ueland. When my son, Jeremy died, Jim came to the funeral. I cried more on him than anyone. We're not fellow coaches – we're brothers. I love him.

**Coaches Jim Musburger and George Bunn** (1972 Bluebook)

The stellar class of '76 were equally gifted in football. Coached by Phil Johnson and Jim Musburger, they won nine conference games consecutively to win Top-of- the- State Football Conference Champions, and then defeated Roseau 23-6 in the conference play-off. After beating McIntosh-Winger 18-6 for the State Semi-Final, the deeply talented Rabbits lost to Esko in the Championship game to place second in State Class C football. Led by co-captains Dan Sele and Mike Kuznia, and seniors Rick Olson, John Downhour, Ron Slaathaug,

Luther Germundson, Jon Nordine, Rod Brown, Dan Clark and Randy Hultgren, the football team put Karlstad on the map. Rick Olson, Luther Germundson, and Dan Clark were all-conference selections. Brian Sele, Ken Wethers, Steve Rowland, Jim Cardinal, Jeff Altendorf, Wayne Lutz, Neil Germundson, Todd Carlson, Ron Austad, and managers Brian and Bruce Wheeler completed the varsity roster.

### Runner-up to State Class C Football 1975-76

**Left to right: Danny Clark, Ron Slaathaug, Mike Kuznia, John Downhour, Danny Sele (holding the trophy), Luther Germundson, Ken Wethers, Randy Hultgren and Todd Carlson.**
(20 November 1975, *North Star News*)

**Wayne Lutz '77** reflects on the championship year: *We went undefeated all the way to the state championship where we lost 62 to nothing against Esko. Esko was a small town similar to Karlstad, but had that year become a consolidated school system incorporating many schools into one. Hence they fell through the cracks and should not have been a Class C, 11-man team like we were. I believe the next year they were moved to Class B, and then the year after that they were moved to Class A. Karlstad should really have been in a 9-man league, but I don't think we had those back then. We had 16 on the team in the picture in the Blue Book, but we'd recruited some kids late in the season to help with practices. Realistically we had maybe 13 players who played, and most of us never left the field, playing both ways and playing the whole game through. Esko on the other hand was substituting players on every play. So we were out classed and beaten badly. But we were Minnesota Class C State Runner-up.*

Karlstad Varsity Football Team 1975-76: Row 1: B. Sele, K. Wethers, J. Downhour, R. Brown, R. Slaathaug, J. Nordine. Row 2: Coach Johnson, R. Olson, S. Rowland, D. Clark, D. Sele, J. Cardinal, Coach Musburger. Row 3: B. Wheeler, manager, J. Altendorf, W. Lutz, M. Kuznia, L. Germundson, N. Germundson, R. Hultgren, B. Wheeler, manager. Absent: T. Carlson and R. Austad
(1976 Bluebook)

**Phil Johnson,** who coached the 1975-76 football to runner-up at state, echoes George Bunn's recall of great area coaches: *When I started teaching and coaching in Karlstad there was a wealth of quality basketball coaches in the immediate area: Jim Musburger, Warren Keller, Louis Deere, Ron Ueland as well as their assistants George Bunn, Gary Schuler and John Schmidt. Later, I was a school administrator in southern, northeast and central Minnesota. I did not understand the quality of these northwest Minnesota coaches until I went elsewhere, that northwestern Minnesota had the largest number of quality coaches in a geographic area. But later, I began to realize that it was true. At first, I was confused by the lack of quality coaches in other areas of the state. It took me two decades to realize that there were good coaches in southeastern Minnesota like John Nett at Winona Cotter and Jerry Snyder at Lake City who each had multiple state championships. I got to know Jerry Snyder (former Middle River coach) while I was a school administrator in southeastern Minnesota. I was sharing an adult beverage with him at the state tournament in 1982. He reassured me that Jim Musburger was the best of the best when it came to coaching* *basketball. Larry Peterson was a quality basketball coach at Roseau in the late 1970s. From Roseau he went to Appleton where he had a tremendous won loss record. In the 1980s Larry and I became very close friends. He told me that Jim Musburger was the best coach he ever coached against, without question. He shared that he used to take Musburger's schemes and put them into practice.*

*I became a better coach by watching Jim's practices. My God were those practices organized with no standing around, and the juniors and the seniors made sure everybody hustled. He had a few basic principles that he coached by: you played man-to-man defense and you had to know the opponent that you were guarding well. If the man-to-man was not working well, then he called a time out and then you worked harder to play better man-to-man. You picked your starting lineup early in the year so that by the end of the year they were a cohesive unit. He had an eye for talent. Sometimes I would sit in the stands at an early season game and think to myself, "Why is he starting him?" By the end of the year, I would think, "I hate that when Musburger is always right." He did not schedule many games before Christmas, then after New Year's you played as many Tuesday, Friday, Saturday games in one week as you could to get ready for the tournaments. He loved Saturday night games because this gave you one more after school practice sometime during the season. He did not take players out quickly when they got in foul trouble. You had to have three fouls in the first half before you went to the bench and four fouls in the third quarter. Sometimes he did not sit you at all, you just had to play better defense.*

*No team played better defense than a Musburger coached team. He kept it simple and basic. Play defense with your feet not your hands, players would often refer to chesting their opponent. Guard the baseline, no excuses, never give up the baseline. Stay between your man and the basket, then get in position to rebound. Oh my, did it ever work. I was an administrator (AD, principal, superintendent) at schools where basketball coaches talked defense and how defense won games, but they did not communicate to the players how to play defense. They did not understand. I worked at schools that won state championships in cross country and track, took second in the state in football, third in baseball, fourth in basketball, ranked first in the state in basketball, supervised coaches who later won state championships and made multiple state appearances, had the top basketball recruit in the state who went on and played in the final four. Some of these coaches were poor, some were average, some were very good, some are in the coach's hall of fame, but no one was in Jim Musburger's class.*

*I was an administrator at a school that had a pretty good basketball team. We were playing in the sectional championship game in Bemidji. Susan and I called Adeline and Jim and invited them out for a meal. They accepted and Jim surprised me by saying we are going to the game with you. Now this was a section basketball championship but neither team played Musburger defense. Jim got his mind into the game and kept expressing concern about the defense as well as on offense, keeping the ball on the perimeter. I watched with amusement how frustrated he was. I am sure he was thinking that most of the teams he coached would have won that night. This also illustrates how small school basketball has changed in Minnesota.*

**Varsity cheerleaders: Carla Oistad, Ann Grandstrand, Carol Vik, Holly Grandstrand, Charlene Helling, and Barb Johnson.** (1976 Bluebook)

## 21. KARLSTAD RABBITS 1976-77

*Coach related to us in our own individual way to put together a team each year ready to compete. Teams today could also learn from him; instead of being more focused on the slam dunk or three-point shot for individual accomplishments and fame. –*
Lowell Swanson '77

The 1977 Varsity basketball team, led by Seniors Neil Germundson, Brad Nelson, Wayne Lutz, Lowell Swanson and Loel Olson (captain and All-Conference), captured a season record of 17 wins and 7 losses. Juniors Brian Bothum, Justin Dagen, Tim Porter and Alan Spilde; Sophomores David Spilde, Mike Poole, Todd Spilde, Tom Porter; and freshmen Rory Anderson and Kevin Kuznia filled out the roster.

Varsity cheerleaders Pam Helling, Vicky Hams, Suzanne Johnson, Charlene Helling, Ann Grandstrand and Ann Germundson led the school spirit.

**Bill Margerum** joined head coach Jim Musburger as assistant coach. Bill recalls his first year in Karlstad: *In 1976, I accepted a teaching position in Karlstad and was lucky to be the assistant coach under Jim. I had no idea how fortunate I was to learn from a master. Jim took me under his wing and accepted me and my "new-fangled ideas," like zone defenses. He never formally sat me down and said that his way was the way to coach. But after that year, I knew that I wanted to be a coach in the same mold as Mr. Musburger and that shaped my future. I do have an olfactory memory of smelling salts that Coach would share with his players in the final huddle before tip-off!*

**David Spilde '79** remembers a Hallock game: *I was a sophomore guard playing Hallock and shot 0 for 9 from the top of the key. During half-time, coach let me have it up one side and down the other in the locker room. On the way back to the gym, he took me aside and said, "Keep shooting, you're bound to start hitting the basket." I went out and hit three in a row.*

Football Coach **Phil Johnson** responds: *Reaming David out and then telling him to keep shooting sounds just like Jim. The team needed to hear the first part, David alone needed to hear the last part.*

**Karlstad Varsity Basketball Team 1976-77: 17 wins, 7 losses
Row 1: D. Spilde, J. Dagen, T. Spilde, R. Anderson. Row 2: B. Nelson, N. Germundson, L. Olson, W. Lutz, L. Swanson. Row 3: Tom Porter, K. Kuznia, Tim Porter, B. Bothum, M. Poole, A. Spilde.**
(1977 Bluebook)

**Loel Olson '77** shares his journey on the Karlstad Varsity basketball team: *My first exposure to Mr. Musburger and District 32 basketball came in the fall of 1965. I was five, we had moved back to the farm in Karlstad from Roseau, and at about that time two things happened that deeply affected the rest of my childhood. John Erickson, a boy four years older whose parents ran the Hartz store where Mom worked, and my cousin, Craig Bolin, introduced me to 1964 Topps baseball cards. I was quickly hooked and eagerly awaited the arrival of "Series 5 and 6" to show up in town sometime in late July or early August. It was always a race between Craig, the Germundson boys, and me to buy up as many of those as possible before they disappeared. The final series every year, "Series 7", never got within an airplane ride of Karlstad.*

The other captivating experience became watching District 32 basketball, especially the 1966 Rabbits win the District 32 championship under Mr. Musburger's guidance. 1966 set the tone for the rest of my school years, and began my connections with the man, who along with other teachers and my family, had the greatest influence on my life. Mr. Musburger and Mr. Heck, the football coach, quickly become familiar to me as my brother, Tim, played for them in his high school years, smack dab in the middle of the VietnamWar/Beatles/Kennedy brothers 1960's. The 1966 District 32 basketball championship was Mr. Musburger's first district championship. Unforgettable are the players and coaches that became Godlike heroes to me during that span: Ernie Pietruszewski, Neil Wikstrom, Neil Skogerboe, David Henry, Tim Nordin and my brother. Their uniforms, white sleeveless home uniforms with **Karlstad** stitched across the front, navy blue with short sleeves for away games, blazingly white Converse/Chuck Taylor shoes... those players were complete magic to watch. I learned that they used white shoe polish to make the shoes look clean. The best player, my brother Tim insisted, was Brian Sjodin, "The best outside shooter I've ever seen."

As a seven-year-old, I watched the presentation of the district All-Conference awards. There stood the most heroic twelve guys on the planet, and I immediately wanted to be one of those All-Conference guys someday. Some were in uniform, sweaty, having just won or lost a huge game, and their facial expressions mirrored the game's result. Others were in street clothes, but everybody important in the world, from every school and town that mattered, was either on the court or in the stands. It became a huge goal of mine to be All-Conference not once, but twice. Those two goals dominated me for the next 10 years.

We moved into town from the farm west of Karlstad around 1966, renting a house on Main Street. My sisters and my brother were excellent students and my brother was a very good athlete. We had some cool cousins, uncles, and aunts in the area. And that's about the total amount of status our family had. We were poor, poor, poor. I started a paper route when I was six, delivering the Minneapolis Tribune every Sunday morning. Dad worked hard at his job, basically staying overnight at whatever dairy farmer's house, maybe a hundred miles from home, where he had spent the afternoon. Mom was a clerk at Hartz, but at $1 an hour, the money wasn't exactly rolling in. I felt, in

*some ways, lower and less worthy than the school kids who had families
that owned a downtown business or a nice farm, families that drove
nice cars and wore nice clothes. I quickly learned that being real smart
in school and being the best athlete possible carved out my status.*

*It turned out that the famous Mr. Musburger was my neighbor, and lived
across the alley in the Wikstrom apartments. His skinny, very tall, very
blond son, Jimmy, was older than me by five years, but we would
occasionally end up in some shared adventure with a bunch of boys
involving churchyard football, 4th of July fireworks, or playing hide and
seek at night in the dark hospital yard across from his house. My
constant companions were Jimmy Nordine and the Germundson boys,
Luther and Neil. We always kept an eye out for John Sollund, local cop,
who would drive up in his faded plumber's pickup and kick us out of the
churchyard. And fifteen minutes later we would sneak back in and take
our chances. We never really figured out why they didn't want us
playing there. Now they've installed a propane tank, presumably on
purpose, right in the middle of the churchyard.*

*Once my father shot a buck, brought it home, and hung it in a tree in our
yard. I ran straight to the one guy who really mattered, and sure
enough, Mr. Musburger came right over to admire the deer. Although
only seven years old, I could tell that Mr. Musburger and Mr. Heck were
held in high esteem by Tim and the other young men on the basketball
and football teams. They were frequently discussed at home, and details
of what they said, how particular games went, and what was going on
with the other players were listened to with great interest. It was a
complete tossup as to whether Musburger, Heck, or JFK were the
greatest Americans of the decade.*

*Actually, that's not completely true. I remember faintly that Tim was in
the "dog house" with one or both of them at some point in his basketball
career. Tim has a tougher streak than me by a long way, could take
criticism, shrug it off, and use it to get better. I sensed as I approached
high school sports that the coaches saw me as a clone of my older
brother, and at first, treated me as they would him. But at some point
the coaches knew that I was as soft as a banana. Criticize me and I
wilted. Praise me and I blossomed. Mr. Musburger's approach was
perfect. The worst thing he ever said was, "Good God, a guy with legs*

*like yours ought to be able to jump six feet off the ground." Not exactly a piercing blow to my ego.*

*As a result, I would do anything for those guys, and loved every minute of it. I worked as hard as I could every minute of practice and games, and then I would play even harder to garner more praise. Coach made a point to tell me frequently, usually privately, to not listen to the critics. "You just keep doing what you're doing. You're doing absolutely great." How he knew that was exactly what I needed is beyond me. Whatever the comments, they were perfect for me and sustained me for years.*

*When I went to college at Crookston I played basketball for two weeks. The coach was a super intense, very hard guy. I don't think I heard a single compliment of any type in those two weeks. After years of total trust and mutual respect with Mr. Musburger and Mr. Bunn, I wilted like a frozen flower. And quit.*

*A truly great thing started about 5th grade. Mr. Musburger organized "intramural basketball" on Saturday mornings. As a teacher now, there is no way I would give up my Saturdays to voluntarily organize 30 snot-nosed 12-year-olds to play basketball. But every Saturday morning an unshaven Mr. Musburger would show up by nine o'clock and organize teams, run the clock and provide heaven to us for the next three hours on the big gym floor. They would even have a scorebook, which we poured over after each game. Those mornings were nuts for absolutely being fun. Play a game, ref a game, play another game, maybe even one more as the less ardent players would drift off and Jimmy Nordine and I could squeeze onto a team a player short before the morning ended. By noon our feet were sore, our socks were wet balls of sweat, and we would leave happy as a bunch of backyard puppies.*

*Karlstad had many excellent teams and players, and I can trace the years with their names. Brian Sjodin, the last remnant of the great 1966 team, with Jack and Greg Oistad, followed by the likes of Lowell Sjodin, Jerry Pietruszewski,, Kent Hanson, and John Oistad. Soon Glen Spilde, Richie Pietruszewski and Chris Johnson were playing. Chris Johnson may have been the only All-Conference player ever who didn't actually start on his team. That was also when a young Jimmy Musburger*

161

*showed up after Lowell Sjodin hurt his knee in the districts. That was an amazingly talented bunch, with height and muscle, depth, and great basketball skills. The years rolled along, and eventually it was Jimmy Musburger leading a team with John Erickson and Ricky Netterlund. The Rabbits faded a bit when Jimmy graduated, but were decent with Tim Johnson and David Grandstrand, Ken Johnson and Ricky Netterlund. All those years I loved watching the B squad and varsity games, and the tournaments were heaven. I remember riding with Loren Germundson and his son's better friends to Stephen after leeching my way into the car, and seeing the long stream of car lights as far as you could see heading to Stephen that evening. As I look back I am amazed at how graceful and perfect so many of the players were in District 32 basketball during those years. On our little planet, these young athletes were often as good as they could possibly be.*

*Back then we practiced close to three hours a day, five days a week. My hero was Lowell Sjodin, a tall smooth Norse God. I guarded him once in a Saturday come-back-to-Karlstad game. There was no way on God's green earth to stop his fade away baseline jumper, and that was years after his high school peak. If he hadn't been injured during the District tournament, I think that team was the one Karlstad team that could have gone to State. He was on the Karlstad Pirate town ball team and pitched us into the state tournament, and I learned he was the sweetest, gentlest fireballer I've ever known.*

*I hated and admired those scowling animals from Argyle. Good god! Press, harass, steal, and rebound... Those little 5'8" *&*&*$@& could box out and out-rebound anybody. Playing against their press was usually a nightmare, yet it felt great if you could actually beat it or control it, as we sometimes did.*

*There is one player that I need to mention Jimmy Nordine was a year older than me and my absolute favorite teammate of all time. He was my friend and neighbor during elementary and junior high years, and I trusted him like no other teammate in the hundreds of baseball, basketball, and football games we were in over the years. As we started to mature, we had a ferociously successful year on the basketball B squad together. Mr. Bunn started teaching us how to full court zone press, and we could really tear some teams apart. Jimmy and I were*

162

guards, often trapping somebody together, and we both loved to fast break after a steal. I remember Mr. Wayne Rud, the Strandquist coach at the time but also our Sunday School teacher, saying that Jimmy was the best guard in the conference. "The best B squad guard?" No, the best guard in the conference, period, was his reply. Jimmy ripped up his knee a few months later in football. He tried to play sports after the injury, but never trusted his knee and quit playing sports. I never thought about it at the time, but that injury not only ripped up his knee; I'm sure it messed up his world. Jimmy died a few years ago in Arizona and my tribute to him is here.

The beginning of every basketball season was tough. No matter how hard you tried, your body was not ready for the intensity of three-hour practices. Blisters quickly formed inside our Chuck Taylors, as we cut and shuffled and flew down the court with intense effort. During drills, there was always a mental moment of, "Oh, my God", followed by a deep breath and a steeling of the mind to hustle and succeed in the drill. And at the end of practice, we would crawl down to the locker room to peel the sweat-soaked, drenched socks off our blistered feet. And then the next day, you would pull on fresh socks over the tender areas and go do it again.

Haircuts were also part of the ritual. We always figured that local barber Jay Spilde and Mr. Musburger had discussed things thoroughly and a basketball haircut was a heinie, [crew cut] or something as close to a heinie as possible. As the 1970's rolled along, this became more and more of an unwanted sacrifice in the era of bell-bottoms, Scooby Do, and Peter Frampton. Then one year, somebody went in, asked for, and got a "basketball" haircut with short bangs, a little length on the sides and back... and apparently Mr. Musburger never said a word. And that was the end of the heinie era. I have a picture from the North Star News of our team sitting on the floor after losing to Argyle in the District finals, and there's not a heinie in sight.

In a few days our bodies and feet would get in reasonable shape, and we would scrimmage somebody, usually Warren, and soon sore feet and heavy breathlessness were a thing of the past. But an exception occurred in the winter of 1973-74. Principal Earl Lutz's response to the Energy Crisis was to limit entrance to the school for practice during

Christmas break. However, we knew which windows on the second floor would slide open, so we climbed up the drains that hung down to the ground, got on the roof on the west side of the school, and sneaked into the gym a couple of times. We didn't dare turn on the gym lights and played in half-darkness before sneaking out.

The second-best feeling in the world was a game day. But the very best feeling in the world was the day of a tournament game. Everything you had worked hard for was happening tonight, the gym would be packed, and whatever happened would be remembered for the rest of your life.

Mr. Musburger has always been one of the funniest guys I've ever met. On a Sunday picnic at Lake Bronson State Park with my family when I was about eight, he happened to be doing the same thing one picnic table away with his family. Excited to have my big brother's coach so near, I showed him a cool rock with a flat side that I had found. "Holy cow, that's a Geographical Phenomenon!" he told me. "Well, look, it's got a flat side!" Genuinely excited, I spent the entire day down at the lake searching for more 'Geographical Phenomenons', dragging each one up several hundred yards to the picnic area for his viewing and approval.

I was only on the bench for one year with the varsity, so I didn't get many chances to see Mr. Musburger interact with fans. But two instances are memorable. We were playing in Fosston, and they had Randy Lindfors, a 6'5" senior center who dominated games. We defeated Fosston earlier in the year at the Thief River Falls Christmas tourney, but a game played later in Fosston was a battle we just couldn't win. Lindfors finished with 28 points. During a brief spell on the bench, I heard the Fosston fans harassing a frustrated Mr. Musburger, telling him to sit down, among other things. He turned to the crowd and said, "Oh, shut up. If you didn't have the big guy you couldn't beat your way out of a wet paper bag." I had never heard that "wet paper bag" phrase before, and thought it was extremely clever. My brother-in-law, Jim Johnson of Hallock, related another story. Jim played for Mr. Musburger years earlier, and he and my sister, Virginia, had bought our entire team several pre-game meals over the years celebrating our tournament successes. As a senior, we were playing Hallock up in Hallock, and they had some really nice players, including Mark Bloomquist, Scott Johnson,

*Bob Roy, and 6'4" Jon Nelson. In the first half we were getting beat, and the referee called a moving screen on one of our larger guys. Mr. Musburger jumped up and yelled at the ref, "Moving screen? How can you call that! He hasn't moved all night!" On his return to the bench he winked at Jim sitting up in the Hallock stands.*

**Coach Musburger** elaborated on the Hallock game: *We were down by 26 points at halftime and the referees from Thief River Falls called us on everything. I gave them holy hell at halftime. Well, in the second half, they called nothing on us! After the game, Perry Pearson, Hallock's assistant coach, commented, "We just can't beat you!"*

**Loel** continues: *He always understated expectations for the team, too. From the North Star News in November 1975: "Coach Jim Musburger was not too enthusiastic about prospects for this year's squad. He pointed to Hallock and Kennedy as being the toughest on the west side of District 32 and looked for Newfolden to be very strong in the east with Baudette as a possible dark horse." We won the conference and the District 32 title that year, finishing 19-6 overall.*

*During that year we played Newfolden in the Herald's "Game of the Week". The Herald wrote in the pre-game coverage: "Musburger said he has been disappointed in the Rabbits' play lately. 'We just can't get untracked,' he said. 'We're not scoring well and we're not rebounding well. And we need more out of our big men'." Maybe in this case the sly motivation was for us. We beat Newfolden 54 to 35, and "big man" Luther Germundson scored 14 points and had 13 rebounds, along with "big man" Mike Kuznia's typical 15-point game.*

*Prior to the '76-77 season, he told the Grand Forks Herald: "Our prospects are poor. We have no experience, shoot poorly, and are slow." We managed a 2nd place finish in the Northern Lights conference and got 4th place in the District, finishing 17- 7. One way or another, he was a master at getting us mentally ready for each opponent. "They'll be hanging from the rafters" was a frequent comment before some of our easier games, letting us know that every little town wanted to beat Karlstad. I can't recall losing any games that we should have won. Occasionally we upset better opponents, and would lose to well-respected teams, but I can't remember a single loss to*

*a clearly weaker opponent. He really knew how to get inside our heads
and get the best out of us in every game.*

*It was the era of tile floor gyms for many of the area teams. Kennedy,
Hallock, Lancaster, Middle River, Strandquist, Humboldt, and other
schools had horrible tile gym floors. For those of you who never played
the game, playing on a tile floor was miserable. Not always slippery, but
it took a certain amount of joy out the game for the players. Some of
those gyms were basically quonsets with four bleacher rows on each
side. My sophomore year, we played Lancaster on a very warm
January day, and condensation started coating the tile gym floor. The
referees were in a quandary, because every time you stopped on your
dribble, your pivot foot would slide a few inches like playing on ice.
They chose to call traveling every time; it had to be an all-time traveling
record. This forced both teams to move at a snail's pace and the game
was a farce. In the 3rd quarter I drove toward the left baseline to go up
for an easy jump shot. My feet never stopped, popped up five feet in the
air, and my head thwacked the tile floor. Halma native and Rabbit
fan Tilden Spilde was so concerned that he ran out on the court to assist
me, and landed on his butt, not his head. At that point, officials
postponed the game, and it was played a week later in normal
conditions. When I got to know them in college, Kennedy players talked
about how in February shin splints would always show up on their team.*

**Coach Musburger** adds: *Lancaster was bad, but Newfolden had the
worst gym, a crackerjack box. Their coach told me, "I don't think you
can beat us here." But we did. Baudette's tiny gym was terrible, too. I
had to sit up on the stage and drop down to the floor to coach. We had
a good gym, but our showers were so terrible that Middle River refused
to use them.*

**Loel** continues: *We had our own share of home court advantages. We
had a red clock that came out before the Great Depression, featuring an
8-minute circular section and a second hand sweeping through at a rate
of one minute per revolution. The colors inside the clock would switch
from white to yellow to red. Opponents never had a clue how much time
was left. Sometimes they would politely ask during a pause in the
action, "God, I can't figure out your clock... how much time is left? " An
accurate answer was impossible.*

*Most gyms in those days had very little space behind the baskets. You needed to prepare to stop very quickly after a fast break lay-up, since the two inches of padding typically hanging on the wall wasn't a lot of help. To actually play where you could go all out on a fast break was a pleasure fans probably never understood. Thinking about our home facilities brings to mind our locker room, clearly the worst locker room I've ever seen. Rats would have loved it. It was small, built of gray concrete, with concrete steps leading down to it, and very low ceilings. Under the concrete steps sat white powder in a mesh basket for athlete's foot prevention. Local "bad boys" typically inserted glass in that. The one toilet and showers often had "deposits" left on the floor by more of the same. Mr. Musburger and Mr. Bunn never once met us down there. They always had us dress and get the heck out of there as fast as possible, and we would meet in the home economics room before games and at half time.*

*Mr. Musburger's basketball tenets, imprinted over the many years of practice sessions, are easily recalled:* **"Work on your shooting!"** **"Don't float! Go straight up on your shot!"** **"Start in close, and work your way out!"** **"Go straight up on your lay-ups!"** **"Get the ball on your fingertips, not in your hand!"** **"Move your feet!"** **"Slide your feet! Don't cross your feet!"** **"Get your hands up [on defense]!"** **"Get your butt down!"** *But the main focus was:* **"Sagging man-to-man...Rock-ribbed defense!"** *We practiced and used this so much that it became second nature.*

**"Always know where the ball is!** **"Always know where your man is!"** **"Help out!"** **"Box out! Box out!"** **"What are you doing? Don't ever give up the baseline!"** *And then, to the big guys:* **"Get the ball to a guard! You've got no business dribbling up the court!"** **"Watch your passes!"** **"That's a bad pass! Don't ever throw a crosscourt pass!"** *The cross-court pass has been forgotten by many teams now. They call it a "skip pass", and it is used a lot these days. Holy Mary, if we threw one of those we heard about it. But my all-time favorite is:* **"Too many passes! Shoot the ball!"**

*My senior year was probably the beginning of the end of the Musburger era. Mr. Bunn had left, returning to North Dakota to farm, and that made things feel enormously different. Argyle, still good but missing a bunch of tough athletes, was moved into a different district. In the not too distant future, schools would be consolidated and intense rivalries would be eliminated. As for Mr. Musburger, I'm guessing he was starting to eye the end of his coaching career.*

*Like my brother Tim, my senior year was simply not going to be a repeat of my junior year, when we each were District 32 champions. The key players were gone. We had lost Mike Kuznia, Danny Sele, Randy Hultgren, and Luther Germundson, and I knew going into the season that a district championship was not going to occur. Kennedy was too good. Rich Deere and Barry Langen had us and Newfolden was too tall. But anyway, for whatever reason, I felt like we could handle Hallock, and we did. Perhaps surprising is that Hallock would beat Kennedy twice during the season, but Kennedy we could not beat. It all was like a rock, paper, scissors game.*

*Strandquist surprised us by taking us into overtime in Karlstad that year, led by a young, tall Steve Brekke, who later moved to Warren, and eventually played at UND. I got poked in the eye at some point in that game, and saw two players, two rims, and two balls the rest of that game. It is memorable because classmate Lowell Swanson, eighth man on our depth chart, made what would today be a 3-pointer from the top of the key in overtime to win the game for us. Looking back, it was a huge win for us, and a great moment for Lowell.*

*The most memorable part of my senior year was a bit strange. What evolved for me was the knowledge that this was my last shot, and I wanted to make every moment a memory. I pushed my body as hard as possible in practice and even harder in games early in the season. I tried to do everything sometimes; man to man the guy bringing the ball up the court, getting every possible rebound, bring the ball up the court, and either score or pass off to a scorer every possession. Then start over by harassing the guy bringing the ball up the court. By Christmas time I never got tired on the court and never did the rest of the year. I could do anything I wanted and not get out of breath. I remember my hands would be cold during the school day, and I had pink dots on my arms and hands all day long. Apparently my heart rate was so low that in a normal situation it pumped so little blood that I was cold all day long!*

168

*The other odd thing was a Zen-like sense that came to me a few times during a few games. I could see what was going to happen before it occurred. I knew when David Spilde or I could steal the ball in a trap, and I could see where the ball would rebound before a shot was taken. It was a super high gear, fueled by confidence that was just strange. In two games, Hendrum in the Thief River Falls Christmas tournament, and against Hallock in Hallock, I found that extra gear, tried to do as much as possible all over the court, and found I could pretty much dictate the game results. In both we were down by an extraordinary number of points but came back to win. In Hallock I fouled out in overtime, and Wayne Lutz scored late in overtime to win the game for us. Wayne was a great track athlete and very good football player, but had joined basketball late. His game was athletic but lacked the smoothness that most of us achieved through years of Mr. Musburger's daily* practice of fundamentals. *But the Hallock overtime, along with a big game in Lancaster, were shining moments for him.*

*And then, one day, it was all over.*

*Mr. Musburger made a point of telling seniors that they were welcome back at practice at any time. Not too many former players took advantage of that offer, and I quickly learned why. I showed up for a practice or two during my freshman year in college, and that's when I knew the magic show was over. My body was no longer in shape to play basketball at the level it had been at in high school. Feet were slow, reactions were late, and exertion created breathlessness. But most of all, the entire point and purpose of the previous twelve years was no longer available. It was replaced by a sense of drifting aimlessly and a longing, not exactly a faint longing, for what had been. While relationships with coaches or former teammates were not severed, they could never be the same. Going to a practice was ultimately and inevitably a sad experience. And while I didn't dwell on it excessively, I knew then that I would miss District 32 basketball a great deal.*

*For twelve years I had a front row ticket to one of the greatest shows on the planet. The Musburger/District 32 show gave me status, pride, joy, and thousands of memories of great teammates, great opponents, great fans, and great coaches. It gave me health and strength, it gave me goals, it gave me confidence.*

**Coach Musburger** shares a humorous incident in '76: *I still laugh about one game with Kennedy in Karlstad. We were tied near the end of the game and the refs gave us one free throw and I thought we should have a one on one. I reached over and pushed the button on the scorer's table to stop the game. The refs did not see me do it, but the Kennedy fans did and went beserk. The refs asked the timekeepers what happened but they all claimed they saw nothing, so the refs blamed the scorers. Kennedy got the ball and won by one point. By the way, the refs were right and we only deserved one free throw.* **Ken Urbaniak** comments: *Kennedy Coach Deere told me that Karlstad was out of timeouts, and all of a sudden, the buzzer at the score table went off. Louis went to the score table to find out what happened and was told that Jim did it.*

**Lowell Swanson '77** reminisces: *Basketball was a different game during those times with no shot clock or 3- point shot and we learned the basics of basketball and life. Coach related to us in our own individual way to put together a team each year ready to compete. Teams today could also learn from him, instead of being more focused on the slam dunk or 3-point shot for individual accomplishments and fame. We could count on the advantage from the old-time clock that was in the new gym, not like today with the 10th of a second being common during the last minute.*

*One of his quotes that sticks with me is, "The shortest distance between two points is a straight line," which taught us geometry and also how to drive to the basket. He was usually serious, but with a good sense of humor needed to put up with a group of growing adolescent boys.*

*The bus trips to neighboring schools were usually inspirational and sometimes challenging. The cold weather and buses in the 1970's (yes, I do miss the 70's) meant the older players always sat in the back near the heater. We made it to the games in snowstorms and cold weather except for one time when the bus froze up and stalled on the way to Argyle. We pulled into a farmyard and Mr. Musburger was allowed to use the phone (no cell phones at that time) to call Mr. Helling. They wisely decided to turn the bus around and postponed the game for that night, as it was around minus 30 degrees and getting colder.*

*On another trip to Thief River Falls for their holiday tournament, the players were excited about getting out of Karlstad on a Friday night. We were playing cards and being rowdy when I pushed Scott Thompson, our faithful manager (now deceased), into one of the side bus windows and he hit his head with a loud bang. We all got instantly quiet, and Mr. Musburger turned around only one time and said we needed to focus on the game, among other things, and we did. We won the tournament that weekend, as we had done in previous years. It was always fun to beat Thief River Falls. That night Mr. Musburger allowed Scott to take some aspirin from the medicine bag the manager always carried around. The coaches were always good to the managers and Scott usually got the first choice of Gatorade, which was cooling out the back door to the gym during practice. Some players even got leftover cake from the school kitchen after practice.*

*Another highlight was a home game at Karlstad and coming from behind to beat Strandquist in two overtimes. Nobody wanted to break the winning streak we had for many years over Strandquist. Also making the region tournament in Grand Forks in 1976 meant the team was treated like royalty, but we missed the state tournament by one game and came in third.*

*I graduated in 1977, and he was the head coach I respected and looked up to during my Jr. and Sr. high years and he also respected the parents and other supporters with high regard. We may not have realized it at the time, but he is considered a coaching talent and genius that we all should have learned more from during the brief time he was our coach.*

Led by seniors David Stusynski, Loel Olson, Jeff Altendorf, Wayne Lutz, Neil Germundson and Steve Rowland, the 1976-77 varsity football team ended with a 2-8 season by defeating Crookston Cathedral and Newfolden. Co-captains Wayne Lutz and Neil Germundson were selected for All-Conference. Varsity players included: Gene LaDoucer, Ron Helling, S. Thompson, Kragh Folland, Ron Austad, Tom Green, Todd Spilde, Jim Cardinal, Wayne Anderson, Tim Porter, Brian Sele, Pat Dudley, Alan Spilde, Ron Austad, Tom Porter, Brian Bothum, Lynn Behl, Jim Coffield, Kevin Kuznia, Mike Cleary, Ryan Bothum, managers Brian and Bruce Wheeler and coaches Johnson and Musburger.

**Karlstad Varsity Football Team 1976-77** (1977 Bluebook)

In 1977, Jim Musburger's peers selected him for their Teacher of the Year.

**Warren Keller,** head basketball coach from Argyle, wrote a letter to the editor at the *North Star News*: *Mr. Musburger is truly deserving of the Teacher of the Year Award. His philosophy on teaching and coaching are of the highest caliber. I have coached against Mr. Musburger's teams for the last eight years and he has always finished the game a true gentleman and good sport. The Karlstad School and community must be proud to have such a fine individual working with their children. (3 February 1977 North Star News)*

**John Keller,** Warren Keller's son, was a young boy when his dad and Musburger were rival coaches: *My dad was a tireless worker, both on and off the court. He wrote constantly –notes of encouragement, letters, and even a column for his hometown newspaper. My mom, an English teacher, would correct his spelling and punctuation. When I was a senior, we lost in districts to Stephen and my dad took out an ad in the Stephen Messenger congratulating the Stephen coach, Mike Wysocki. I remember sitting in the coach's room with dad and his assistant, John*

*Schmidt, and Jim Musburger's name came up over and over. He was the one guy my dad looked up to and Dad admired how prepared, both physically and mentally, Musburger's athletes were for each game. Writing a book was on my dad's bucket list, but he died too young.*

**Coach Keller getting a victory ride from his players (arm around Gayle Stoltman) after a thrilling victory over Karlstad in the 1975 District 32 Championship Game in the MCC gym.**
(*Grand Forks Herald*, files of John and Sharon Keller)

**Warren Keller, Argyle Coach (1969-1992)**
**February 9, 1941 – August 30, 2011**

## 22. KARLSTAD RABBITS 1977-78

*During rebound practice under the offensive basket, I would get the rebound, bring the ball down, and Coach would stop the practice and say, "Porter, are you pumping water? Go straight up and make the basket, when you get the rebound, don't bring it down like you are pumping water."* – Tim Porter '78

Varsity basketball team members in 1978 included co-captains Brian Bothum and Tim Porter, Justin Dagen, Brian Sele, Alan Spilde, David Spilde, Troy Spilde, Tom Porter, Gene LaDoucer, Paul Anderson, Mike Poole, Kevin Kuznia, Ron Helling, Kragh Folland, Rory Anderson and managers Mark Minske and Kristen Sandberg. Todd Pack joined Jim Musburger as assistant coach. Tim Porter and Brian Bothum were named all-conference.

**Karlstad Rabbits Varsity Basketball 1978: Row 1: M. Minske, manager, J. Dagen, T. Spilde, Kristen Sandberg, manager. Row 2: T. Spilde, A. Spilde, T. Porter, B. Bothum, T. Porter, D. Spilde. Row 3: Gene LaDoucer, P. Anderson, M. Poole, K. Kuznia, R. Helling, K. Folland, R. Anderson.** (1978 Bluebook)

Varsity cheerleaders were Pam Helling, Ann Germundson, Suzanne Johnson, Carolyn Wikstrom, Polly Anderson and Ann Grandstrand.

Kennedy defeated Hallock 64-48 to tie Strandquist for conference co-champion honors. Earlier in the season, the Rabbits had defeated Kennedy 52-41 in a surprising upset. In the opening round of District 32 play, Grygla defeated the Rabbits 54-47. Kennedy edged Roseau 48-45 to win the district title.

**Kevin Kuznia '80** remembers his first varsity game: *I had the privilege of watching Coach Musburger coach good teams and players when I was still in grade school. By the time I was a freshman, I felt so proud to dress for varsity and sit at the end of the bench. I had so much respect for him and he was a great coach and mentor to me. When he looked down to the end of the bench and called me over to sit next to him, I thought, here's my chance. He put me in the game against Stephen in Stephen. I was so nervous that when I got to the free throw line to shoot, I shot an air ball.*

Coach Musburger ended the year playing a game that had special meaning in his career. On February 7, 1978, Jim Durkin from the *Grand Forks Herald* attended the basketball game in Alvarado where Coach Jim Musburger and his Karlstad Rabbits took on the Alvarado Indians coached by his son, Jimmy Musburger. Durkin wrote that although the older coach discouraged his son from teaching and coaching, Jimmy followed in his dad's tennis shoes. The elder **Musburger** stated, "*When you coach you have to be a disciplinarian, and I thought that would be hard for him. And not only that, if you are sensitive to criticism, you shouldn't be in it. Jimmy lived in the gym and was always athletically minded. But it wasn't easy coaching him. We had some pretty tough encounters. There were many times when we did not talk to each other for a day or two.*

**Jimmy** agreed. "*I lived with the idea of him always telling me what to do. And it was tough on him because he felt he had to get on me more than anybody else. I think I aged ten years in the three he coached me.*"

In the end the younger coach did not get the win. Karlstad defeated the Indians 45-44 in overtime on a free throw by David Spilde, the only point scored in the extra period. *"I'll never get another shot at him, that's what makes me mad,"* lamented Jim Jr. *"It was a once in a lifetime opportunity."*

David Spilde remembered that Coach said that he really didn't care who won the Alvarado game but 'we knew.'

**Tim Porter '78** recalls the Alvarado game: *This was my first big moment, we were playing Alvarado and yes, the opposing coach was little Jim! Luther, our starting center, was hurt, so I started at center, my first time starting on the A team. I remember coach telling us how much this game meant to him. I felt like it was emotional for him, he wanted to win but looking back, I think secretly he was pulling for little Jim. I played, not spectacular, but I played. It was an exciting game that we won in overtime.*

*From very early on, starting in 7th and 8th grade, everyone in my family talked about coach and how great he was. I remember going to games and watching the team play including Jimmy, Kent, Lee Sele, Danny (Moose) Sele and more. The team was good, and I was infatuated with basketball. I certainly remember the year we won district, when Danny Sele stole the ball from a Kennedy player in the last seconds to make a layup and win the game. I wanted more than anything to play for coach. At the same time, coach had open gym on Saturday mornings. It was always a good turnout and of course, coach was there working with us. Then it was time for, "mass basketball," everything goes, kind of like basketball football. I think coach took an interest in me. Those were fun Saturdays.*

*Then in 9th grade I was on the B team and this is where I learned how to play the game - drills, medicine balls, jumping rope, suicide wind sprints, layup drills, long passing, bounce passing and "man to man" defense. Coach said, 'you are a wolf-pack, bend at the knees, follow the ball, sag and help out.' Coach always had great defense. Luther, Danny Sele, Loel Olson, Mike Kuznia, Randy Hultgren are the teammates I remember. It was a good team during my 10th grade year.*

*Some of the random memories from those times that stick out are salt pills, who knew, smelling salts and ankle sprains. Coach would say tape it up and get back out there. During rebound practice under the offensive basket, you would get the rebound, bring the ball down, and Coach would stop the practice and say, "Porter, are you pumping water, go straight up and make the basket, when you get the rebound, don't bring it down like you are pumping water." He would also say, "No rest for the wicked," and sometimes he would make me run the whole practice. I wasn't always in the best shape.*

*It was an honor to play for Coach. After our very last game that we lost in the tournament, I remember coach coming up to me and putting his arm around me. He whispered to me that other than his own son Jim, I was the best center he coached. Not sure if that was true but it meant a lot to me over the years.*

**Todd Pack** remembers his first year of coaching: *I was a first-year teacher/coach at Karlstad in 1977 when I was given the opportunity to be Coach Musburger's assistant coach. I was wet behind the ears and was grateful to have been the assistant where I could learn from the best. When I reflect back over my first years as a coach, I respected and appreciated what I learned from not only Jim Musburger, but from the likes of the North Country legends like: Ron Ueland (MCC), Louise Deere (Kennedy), Gary Schuler (Warren), Warren Keller (Argyle), Ron Omerza (LOW), Eldon Sparby (Middle River), Brian Sage (Warroad), Larry Peterson (Roseau) and I can't leave out Gary Cook, who was in charge of the Karlstad feeder (elementary) program for many years and later became my assistant coach. I am very thankful for the knowledge these coaches shared, not only about basketball, but expectations of the student-athletes and about how to develop a program that is sustainable over time.*

*The Godfather of basketball in District 32 was Jim Musburger. Jim was meticulous with how he went about his business on the court from practices to game preparation, to motivating athletes, as well as showing compassion in his relationship with his players. He was well respected by all opposing coaches and players alike. Thinking back and reflecting on how I would have run my practices as a first-year coach without the experience of actually preparing a practice before, I would have been lost. When I became a head coach, I followed what the best did; I used many of Jim's drills, offenses and defensive schemes. I used his 1-3-1 zone offense many years beyond my time in Karlstad. It was a simple offense, but effective and successful for many of my teams. He had his athletes working hard in practice and was motivational during the game when he felt a player was not putting forth the best effort. His student/athletes always responded after a little chewing out. They both knew as athletes they could do a better on the court. I was always amazed at how he could get the most of his athletes. He had athletes that may not have been as talented as some of our opponents, but he always had them prepared for the battle and they gave their best for him. Defensively, Jim never wanted the opponent to take the baseline! As he would say, that is a Cardinal sin. He was always quick to compliment you. He never thought about just his varsity team. He thought about the program, the athletes and successes, whether that was a win or a learning experience. This was true at the "B" squad level too.*

*A couple other thoughts about Jim as a coach. He would always tell me to go and talk to the officials about a call they made or to watch for a holding, or a violation, which he thought they were missing against our opponent. He would tell me: "You go talk to the officials, they don't like me". I would just laugh. I do not know if he just wanted me out of the huddle during the timeout or he actually thought I would make a difference with the officials. Either way, I had the discussion.*

*I was also there to see father-son coach against each other. Jim Jr. was the head coach in Alvarado/Oslo. We traveled there for the game. I remember Jim being nervous and excited at the same time. It was a great game coached by two great coaches. The players played hard and in the end, Father prevailed over Jr. It was a great night to remember. He knew his opponents and coaches when it came to preparing his game plan and strategies for game situations. Obviously, that comes with his years of experience and coaching against these legends for the number of years Jim did. We were playing Lake of the Woods in Karlstad and we were ahead by one. LOW had the ball for a chance at a last second shot to win the game. There was a timeout. He got in the huddle and drew out what LOW was going to run. The ball was on the side, he said there would be a double staggered screen down low and this player, a red head named Robinson, is going to get the ball and shoot from the baseline. He gave our players the defensive action he wanted as the timeout ended. Okay, I was amazed. LOW came out, ran exactly what Jim had drawn out and we defended as described and went on to win the game by one.*

The 1977-78 football varsity team lost to East Grand Forks Sacred Heart 30-0 for the season opener and went on to end their season with a conference record 4-5. Varsity players included Mark Minske, Ron Austad, Alan Spilde, Gene LaDoucer, Tom Green, Kragh Folland, Ron Helling, Dave Spilde, Richard Bothum, Wayne Anderson, Tim Porter, Brian Sele, Jim Coffield, Ron Kalinowski, Brian Bothum, Tom Porter and Mike Cleary, coached by Phil Johnson and Jim Musburger. Ron Austad and Brian Bothum (co-captains) were named to the Top of the State All-Conference team.

**Karlstad Varsity Football Team 1977-1978: Front Row: M. Minske, R. Austad, A. Spilde, G. LaDoucer, T. Green. Row 2: K. Folland, T. Oistad, R. Helling, D. Spilde, R. Bothum, W. Anderson, Coach Johnson. Row 3: T. Porter, B. Sele, J. Coffield, R. Kalinowski, B. Bothum, T. Porter, M. Cleary.** (1978 Bluebook)

# 23. KARLSTAD RABBITS 1978-79

*I remember sitting on the bench as a freshman, and Coach calling me down to sit next to him. Coach was getting pretty worked up during this game and one of my teammates on the court made a bad pass. He turned to me and asked, "Why would he make that pass?" I was scared and a little nervous, but when I looked at Coach, I noticed a drop of blood running down his forehead. As he wiped his forehead, he saw the blood and said, "Now look, he's making my head bleed, you better get in there so this bleeding stops."* – Tom Porter '79

Jim Musburger coached his final basketball team in 1978-79 with assistant coach Todd Pack. Twenty-five boys reported for basketball and varsity players included co-captains David Spilde and Tom Porter, Troy Spilde, Todd Spilde, Mike Poole, Kragh Folland, Rick Cleary, Kevin Kuznia, Rory Anderson, Gene LaDoucer, David Spilde, Todd Porter and Ron Helling.

The Rabbits claimed the west half of the District 32 title with wins over Greenbush and Hallock and a perfect 7-0 conference record. As the West's No. 1 team, they won a bye in the first round of the district tournament but fell to the Badger Rockets in the opening round with a late rebound basket 45-44. Troy Spilde, David Spilde and Kevin Kuznia led scoring for the Rabbits and Bob Dostal poured in 21 for the Rockets. David recalls Ryan Modahl going over his back to win the game. David Spilde was named to the All-District team. That year, Lake of the Woods defeated Hallock 41-31 for the district title. (1 March, 1979, *North Star News*)

**David Spilde '79** recalls practice: *Practices were hard, fun, and simple but done to perfection. During one practice, a team member made several baskets in a row and coach noticed. He shouted, "Somebody better guard him – he's hotter than a two-peckered goat! The whole team cracked up and I still laugh about it to this day.*

The era of cheerleaders ended this year as girls traded in their cheerleading skirts for basketball and volleyball uniforms.

180

Karlstad Varsity Basketball Team 1978-79: K. Sandberg, Manager, T. Spilde, T. Spilde, M. Poole, K. Folland, R. Cleary, K. Kuznia, R. Anderson, G. LaDoucer, D. Spilde, T. Porter, R. Helling, T. Porter. (1979 Bluebook)

**Tom Porter '79,** writes his story: *I was truly blessed to have the opportunity to be coached by one of the best basketball coaches in Northern Minnesota. Coach stressed the basics of ball handling and correct skills of the game, all to become the best player you could be. Coach pushed you to be the best version of yourself, and he wouldn't let you, as a player, settle for anything less than your best. One day during practice, the team was playing a scrimmage, and I was playing forward. As a shot went up and I went for the rebound, a smaller teammate took the ball from me and started a fast break down the floor. Coach blew the whistle and yelled across the court at me, and told me only the way coach could, "You have arms like tree trunks, you grab that ball and you* *put it back up. You don't put it down on the floor, you shoot it right back up." Then in true Coach Musburger fashion, he came over and showed me exactly what he wanted. What he taught me was a simple way to receive and shoot a rebound, but it was a lesson I used in my game from that day forward.*

*Coach said and did a lot of things, but the one thing that has stuck with me for all these years, that I find myself telling my grandkids in all their endeavors is: Don't cheat yourself, don't get into bad habits, and do things right. This not only applied to me as an athlete, it applied to life itself, and I hope my own kids and grandkids realize the truth in those words and take them to heart, just like I did when Coach said them to me. Playing for this special Coach are some of the best memories I have from Karlstad High School.*

*There is a quote that says: "A good coach can change a game. A great coach can change a life." For me this couldn't be truer about my High School Basketball Coach. As a not so young man, when I get together with some friends for a pick-up game, all those drills and coaching techniques come back to me. I am mainly the one who just waits by the hoop, and plays the rebound, but I still use my tree trunk arms, to keep the ball up and away. I can't recall if I ever had the chance to thank coach for the honor of playing for him, so I'll do it now. Thank you coach for the basketball and life skills I learned while playing under you.*

The varsity football team, led by co-captains Tom Porter and David Spilde, included: Brad Cook, Jimmy Peterson, Mark Minske, Stuart Minske, Robert Sylskar, Gene LaDoucer, Tom Green, Troy Spilde, Todd Spilde, Terry Sonju, Troy Oistad, Kragh Folland, Richard Bothum, Richard Cleary, Ron Kalinowski, Kevin Kuznia, Todd Porter, Ron Helling, Harry Hultgren and managers Chris Olson and Chris Johnson.

The season record ended 2-7 with wins over Greenbush and Benedict.

Tom Porter and David Spilde were named to the All-Conference team.

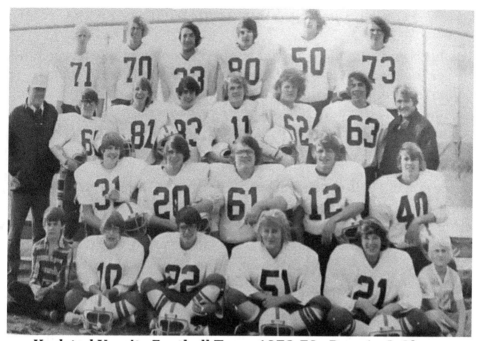

Karlstad Varsity Football Team 1978-79: Row 1: C. Olson, manager, B. Cook, J. Peterson, M. Minske, S. Minske, C. Johnson, manager. Row 2: R. Sylskar, G. LaDoucer, T. Green, T. Spilde, T. Spilde. Row 3: Coach Musburger, T. Sonju, T. Spilde, T. Oistad, K. Folland, R. Bothum, R. Cleary, Coach Johnson. Row 4: R. Kalinowksi, K. Kuznia, T. Porter, R. Helling, T. Porter, H. Hultgren. (1979 Bluebook)

At the end of the season, Coach Musburger signed David Spilde's 1979 yearbook: *Every Coach desires to have a dedicated athlete like you. I wish to thank you for your hard work through these many years. Our total basketball record over the last three years has been 41-21. We have had three winning seasons in a row. I will miss you next year, but best wishes in all your future endeavors. Mr. Musburger*

## 24. FALL 1979: END OF THE JIM MUSBURGER ERA

*You had the ability to bring out the best in all of us. We weren't tall or fast but we were fundamentally superior to many of our opponents and conditioned to give maximum effort for the entire game. You gave a lot back to all of us who were privileged to be coached by you. Thank you for everything you've done – I'll never forget it.* – Kragh Folland '80

At the end of 1979, Coach Musburger hung up his whistle and his tennis shoes to head south to Thief River Falls to work as a driver's examiner for the state. Before he left halfway through the school year, he assisted head coach Phil Johnson with the varsity football team that fall.

The Rabbits, led by co-captain and quarterback Kragh Folland, surprised the Roseau Rams 28-18 in the season opener and then downed Sacred Heart 30-0 before losing to Stephen 25-0, helped by Bill Zemanski's three touchdowns. Their season record 5-4 ended on a winning note with a victory over Greenbush 23-8. Gene LaDoucer (co-captain) and Ron Helling were named to the Top of the State All-Conference team. Gene was also named most valuable player for the conference.

Karlstad Varsity Football Team 1979-80: Row 1: M. Minske, R. Walker, L. Englund, J. Grandstrand, K. Lutz, S. Wikstrom, D. Bernard, B. Cook, S. Minske, T. Spilde. Row 2: Coach Johnson, T. Green, G. LaDoucer, D. Nordine, R. Cleary, R. Sylskar, K. Kuznia, T. Porter, R. Helling, R. Bothum, K. Folland. (1980 Bluebook)

**Seniors: Row 1: Mark Minske, Todd Porter, Kevin Kuznia, Ronald Helling, Kragh Folland, Row 2: Richard Bothum, Thomas Green, Troy Spilde, Gene LaDoucer** (1980 Bluebook)

On November 15, 1979, **Dane Nordine** wrote about the end of the Jim Musburger era: *The high school basketball season gets under way in the area as usual...as usual with one exception. The dean of the area's basketball coaches is missing from the active scene. Through the years, he's claimed 316 basketball victories with his teams and he's lost 163 games. He took teams to the District Tournament finals on seven occasions, once in 1960 with the Strandquist Warriors and the other six times with the Rabbits. His teams captured three District Championships in 1966, 1970 and 1975; they were runners-up six times and they collected third place finishes on five other occasions. This writer cannot remember a year that a Musburger-coached team was not in the thick of the battle right to the end of the season. Time marches on, and like everything else, high school basketball in this area will continue without the coaching of Jim Musburger. Karlstad will likely continue to have fine coaching and remain a formidable foe in this district, but all the same, one can't help but wonder if an opposing coach here and there won't breathe just a little easier when they find Jim Musburger missing from the end of the Rabbit bench. (NSN)*

When **Loel Olson** read Dane's story in the newspaper, he was an exchange student in Scotland. He wrote to the paper: *Mom sends me the North Star News every week. It is nice to see Bubba's Korner back again! I also enjoyed the special basketball season section, especially the Jim Musburger article. I grew up during his coaching era, and*

© Deane Johnson

*vividly remember his teams from 1966 onward. He coached half of my boyhood idols: Lowell and Brian Sjodin, the Pietruszewski brothers, Kent Hanson, Jimmy Musburger, even my brother, Tim. And of course, I know all the recent players from my own Gatorade stealing basketball days. "Yucatan gum!" It will never seem the same to me to see a KHS team not coached by "the old bear." I remember calling him worse things in moments when oxygen was precious, but I will always respect and admire my coach, Mr. Musburger. (13 December 1979 NSN)*

**Middle River center Mike Carriere blocked a shot by Karlstad forward Loel Olson during District 32's basketball tournament semifinal game played at Newfolden. Rick Rantanen (52) and Elwin Ness of Middle River watched the action. The Rabbits defeated the Skippers 63-53.**
(11 March 1976, *North Star News*)

**Chad Rud and Brandon Bergeron with Coach Musburger**
(15 November 1979, p. 17, *North Star News*)

**Jimmy Musburger '72** had a complicated relationship with his dad, the coach. They often locked horns during practices and at home. Looking back 47 years later, Jimmy relishes the good: *Basketball in Karlstad was the highlight of the school year. We loved our other sports but basketball was king. The community supported us enthusiastically and we were treated like royalty. Dad was responsible for building the winning culture and he was considered the best coach in northern Minnesota. I remember the interview in the Grand Forks Herald with Minnesota State High School League Hall of Fame Coach Warren Keller. He was asked what people had the greatest influence on his coaching philosophy. He went on to list college legends John Wooden, Bobby Knight, and one high school coach named Jim Musburger. The good coaches tried to emulate dad's program. I have coached basketball for thirty years and can honestly say I have been successful because of dads teaching. I stressed the same fundamentals, discipline, work ethic, and teamwork that dad taught.*

*I had the opportunity to coach against dad the year I taught in Alvarado. The Grand Forks Herald did a huge article about the game with several photos. It was a classic between two average teams. Dad managed to pull out the victory in overtime. Dad and I had to be on our best behavior because mom was in the audience. It was so much fun and I think our teams mirrored each other in effort, fundamentals and style. I was privileged to coach against a legendary coach.*

*What do I recall about dad in high school? First of all dad was a master motivator. He had the ability to maximize potential in all of his players. Many times we were not the most talented, but we won because we were the best schooled, conditioned and coached. I recall not fearing any team because our culture conditioned us to believe we could defeat any opponent. I can't recall being defeated soundly by anyone. We were always competitive and opponents gave their best effort because of our reputation.*

*Practices were hard but fun. I looked forward to practice every day. I can see dad in his khakis, windbreaker jacket, tennis shoes and whistle. We were expected to give our best and do skills correctly. Repetition, repetition, repetition. Do it right or we would continue on until we did it right. We started practice shooting on our own and we had better be* working or else. I remember Chris Johnson running after his shot like a bat out of hell. We would get exhausted just watching him. He would also give play by play of each shot. I remember running if we missed a lay-up so we missed very few.

Dad was a disciplinarian and we did not want to displease him. All players respected him as a coach and person. When we were disciplined, we knew we deserved it. The players knew that dad cared about them as people. Any successful coach has that attribute and dad was a player's coach.

I remember in my senior year the semi-finals of the district tournament. Our starting team consisted of John Erickson, Jerry Olson, Mark Sang, David Vik, and myself with Tim Johnson and Bob Johnson the first players off the bench. We had a great year even though we were not the most talented team in the district. We led the whole way and looked like we were on our way the finals. We were leading by one point with a few seconds remaining when Newfolden made a bad pass and the ball was going out of bounds. One of the officials happened to get in the way and stopped the ball. Newfolden retained possession and threw up a Hail Mary to beat us by a point. We were devastated by the loss. I will never forget that.

I remember the meals bought for us by community members and the after game get- togethers at Tilden and Shirley's home. The pep fests before every game (something that is rare now) was a magical time for all of us.

After practice, John, Bob, and I would enter the school kitchen through a vent above the door. We would feast on Irene Bolin's apple crisp and drink milk from the milk machine. This practice continued until we were caught and warned of dire consequences if we did it again. Dad would give us a pass out of study hall to go to the coach's room and hang out (ostensibly to wash and fold towels, according to John Erickson). There was a time when we would play ping-pong on the stage until we got caught and that ended that. I remember showering after practice for half an hour. We had some of our best conversations amongst the salamanders, frogs, snakes, and mold.

*Dad was a Hall of Fame coach if he had coached longer. I have seen and worked with many excellent teachers and coaches and dad is at the top. Those were great times and hard to believe it's been 47 years.*

*Dad and I have relived his coaching years many times over the decades. He remembers everything about every game and every player. I have never heard him say a negative word and am amazed at his ability to bring out the best in his players. He taught not only basketball, but how to be good people.*

**NO HARD FEELINGS...Karlstad Rabbits coached by Jim Musburger vs. the Alvarado Indians coached by Jim Musburger, Jr. The Rabbits prevailed 45-44 in overtime.**
(*Grand Forks Herald,* 8 February 1978, p. 2D)

**Jeff Musburger '65,** Jim's brother, shares Bemidji memories: *I was a freshman in 1961 at Bemidji High School when I started basketball. The varsity practiced in the old gym in our big school. I moved to varsity my sophomore year and was sent to see the coach in the coach's room. All the pictures of the former basketball teams lined the hallway on the way to the coach's room. There hung the picture of the 1948 basketball team, the team that won the state championship, with the picture of my brother Jim. I am 15 years younger than my brother and my family never talked about sports, so I knew nothing about my brother's team. My brother's success inspired and motivated me to work very hard on the basketball team.*

*After I graduated from high school, Jim visited our family in Bemidji and we sat down and put together all the plays that Bemidji used in their basketball program. When Jim's Karlstad team defeated Bemidji, he used a lot of the plays and I know Phil Bunn, the Bemidji coach, knew exactly what was going on. Jim and I probably weren't the best players, but we worked so hard to be the best we could for our team. Jim was a character, always up to something. He would tease the older boys and they would chase him to give him a good beating, but he would run into the Catholic Church to hide.*

**Julie Musburger Hoppe '81** shares favorite memories: *Dad and I spent a lot of time together. I remember walking many days to school with him at 6:00 in the morning – he was always the first one to arrive at school. He would put me to work, correcting papers and writing on the chalkboard. But what I really loved was hanging out in the coach's room with him, eating vitamin C tables and helping him wash basketball uniforms. I had the honor of being the Rabbit mascot in full rabbit costume, which was always fun except when Stephen fans threw raisins at me!*

*I also recall Kenny Johnson and Dave Vik playing ball with me when I was a little kid. I loved going to the gym with dad on Saturday mornings – all the happy, sweaty, screaming kids created a great scene. But my all-time favorite was to watch mom and dad embrace on the court floor after his wins. I was so excited when the football team went to state in Walker in 1976 – that was a special experience for our team and community. So many great memories!*

A Friday afternoon pep fest before the 1970 Regional Tournament: Varsity cheerleaders with "Miss Rabbit" Julie Musburger and "Little Cheerleader" Natalie Dagen
(12 March 1970, North Star News)

Marna Bothum, Julie Musburger, Stacey Sandberg, Vicki Hams
(1976 Bluebook)

192

**Jim and Adeline Musburger, 1970 District 32 Championship game** (12 March 1970 *North Star News)*

# Karlstad 1980 Blue Book Dedication to Jim Musburger
(1980 Bluebook)

On August 30, 1988, Dane Nordine pondered Jim Musburger's legacy nine years later: *Jim coached the Karlstad team for 23 years and coached at Strandquist for five years prior to that time. Trouble is, he was such a good coach and successful one during his tenure here in Karlstad, that many fans have trouble forgetting him, and that makes it tough for any new coach to take over the reins of the Rabbit fortunes. He's been gone awhile now, and give it about another generation, and maybe our coaches won't any longer have to be compared with the red head from Bemidji.* (30 August 1988, *North Star News*)

***There isn't anyone who coaches like him anymore.***
– Paul Bostrom'67

## 25. THE LAST WORD BY COACH JIM MUSBURGER

I was lucky to have great coaching at Bemidji High School. After completing ninth grade at the lab school at Bemidji College, I started my sophomore year at Bemidji High School. I made the B squad and my coach, Glen Barnum, had played for the University of Minnesota. He stressed sound fundamentals and superb conditioning. Coach Barnum mentored me and taught me so much about basketball.

One of the highlights of my life, and I've had many, was winning the Minnesota State Basketball title my senior year on March 20, 1948. We defeated Hopkins 38-29 at the University of Minnesota Field House before a crowd of 16,000 fans. A procession of 200 cars stretching for ten miles escorted us from Cass Lake. Prior to our arrival, all the telephone operators each took a page of the telephone directory and called every name on it to have them ready to meet us at the high school for a celebration. At that time, we had only one class of basketball so this was a big deal. Our practices were very competitive as basketball was the only winter sport and king pin in Bemidji. We played all our games at the college gymnasium – and all the games were packed. We would sneak into the high school and college gyms on Sunday afternoon to play ball. Even the golf course had a hoop, where I and the other caddies would pass the time between rounds.

I've had a lot of support over the years. George Bunn really knew his basketball and was a great assistant coach. Coaches from surrounding towns, including Wally Boen, Louis Deere, Warren Keller, Ron Ueland and Jim Schindele, were great competitors and friends. Also, I had a salesman come to the school to sell athletic shoes and equipment, and he had played college ball. He would help me with defensive plays and other coaching tactics. But my boys, my players, they are the ones who have brought me whatever success I've enjoyed. They were fundamentally sound, completely dedicated to the team and could run all night. Why, Chris Johnson could jump rope forever, sideways, backwards – he was the best! And who can forget the fans? You cannot get better fans than at Strandquist and Karlstad. Why, one year everybody chewed Yucatan gum, just because I did.

We built a team from the ground up. Over 25 elementary boys would show up for basketball practice every Saturday morning. We needed two gyms so Karl Carlson would take one gym to help me out with the games.

I've enjoyed every team that I coached over the years. Both the 1958 and 1959 Strandquist teams took us to the district semifinals, and the 1960 team played for the district championship in thrilling tournament play. We only had a couple dozen boys in the entire high school, but they were stellar athletes and great kids. The hospitality of that small town to my family will never be forgotten.

If I had to choose the best Karlstad team, the '66 team made the least mistakes – at least until they got to the region. The talented 1970 team took us again to the regions, but 1974 had to be the most exciting season. We edged Stephen in overtime 59-51 to win the sub-district tournament and then upset Roseau 62-61 and Kennedy 45-44 in the semi-finals before losing to Argyle 60-50 in the finals. The 1975 season had the most heartbreaking loss to Argyle in the district finals. Once again in 1976 we headed to the regionals by defeating Baudette, a much bigger team, 39-38, to clinch the championship.

I had a great run. I gave it my all.

**\*On October 12, 2019, Jim Musburger will be inducted into the Minnesota State High School Coaches Association Hall of Fame.**

*There was always respect and a bit of awe in his presence.* –
Conrad Lubarski '69, Strandquist and Argyle

**Reunion with Ernie Pietruszewski, Coach Jim Musburger, Brian Sjodin and Lowell Sjodin, 22 November 2014.**
(Photo courtesy of Ernie Pietruszewski)

**1966 50th Class Reunion 2016: David Henry, Coach Jim Musburger, Neil Skogerboe, (**Photo courtesy of David Henry)

# WORKS CITED

Bemidji High School Yearbook. *Lumberjack 1948.* Lumberjack Staff. Print. Printed by The Northland Times.

Bengtson, Harlan. Email to author, 22 May 2019.

Benson, Neal. Email to author, 5 April 2019.

Boen, Chester. Letter to author, 16 April 2019.

Bostrom, Paul. Letter to author, 9 February 2019.

Bunn, George. Letter to author, 22 December 2018.

Carlson, Karl. Letter to author, 22 December 2018.

Clark, Dan. Letter to author, 14 January 2019.

Dagen, Troy. Email to author, 15 January 2019.

Durkin, Jim. "The Musburger Coaches." *Grand Forks Herald*, 8 February 1978.

Erickson, John. Phone interview with author, 13 December 2018, Email to author, 29 December 2018.

Erickson, Mark. Letter to author, 24 April 2019.

Folland, Kragh. Letter to Jim Musburger, 7 October 2010.

Grandstrand, David. Email to author, 8 February 2019.

Hanson, Kent. Emails to author, 24 December 2018, 5 April 2019.

Heck, Duane. Phone interview with author, 13 April 2019.

Henry, David. Letter to Jim Musburger, 16 June 2016. Email to author, 16 October 2018.

Hoppe, Julie Musburger. Email to author, 10 February 2019.

Hultgren, Randy. Phone interview with author, 28 November, 1 December 2018.

Jeanotte, Sheila Nordine. Email to author, 18 October 2018.

Johnson, Ken. Email to author, 8 May 2019.

Johnson, Chris. Phone interview with author, 16 May 2019.

Johnson, Jim. Email to author, 1 May 2019.

Johnson, Phil. Email to author, 18 March 2019.

Karlstad High School Yearbook. *Blue Book 1963.* Mary Folland and Staff. Print.

Karlstad High School Yearbook. *Blue Book 1964, Blue Book 1965, Bluebook 1966* Blue Book Staff. Print. American Yearbook Company; Hannibal, MO.

Karlstad High School Yearbook. *Blue Book, 1967, Blue Book, 1968, Blue Book 1969.* Blue Book Staff. Print. Archives, Karlstad High School.

Karlstad High School Yearbook. *Blue Book, 1970. Blue Book, 1971.*

Blue Book Staff. Print. Paragon Yearbooks.

Karlstad High School Yearbook. *Blue Book, 1972, 1973, 1974, 1975, 1976, 1977, 1978, 1979, 1980..* Blue Book Staff. Print. Friesen Yearbooks; Altona, Manitoba.

Kasprowicz, Betty. Email to author, 30 May 2019.

Kasprowicz, Richard. Email to author, 20 May 2019.

Keller, John. Phone interview with author, 13 June 2019.

Krantz, Randy. Letter to author, 19 March 2019.

Kuznia, Kevin. Email to author, 31 March 2019.

Kuznia, Mike. Email to author, 8 January 2019.

Larson, Doug. Email to author, 17 December 2018.

Lubarski, Conrad. Phone interview with author, 7 April 2019. Letter to author, 15 April 2019. Email to author, 1 June 2019.

Lutz, Wayne. Email to author, 28 March 2019.

Lyons, Bob. "Hot Shooting Karlstad Edged by East Side 60-56." *Grand Forks Herald*, 28 January 1970.

Margerum, Bill. Letter to author 15 January 2019.

Moen, Richard. Letter to author, 29 March 2019.

Morlan, Cliff. "Jacks' Cagers Spill Thief River, Upset by Karlstad." *Bemidji Pioneer,* 12 January 1970.

Musburger, Jeff. Phone interview with author, 28 March 2019.

Musburger, Jim Jr. Email to author, 4 February 2019.

Musburger, Jim Sr. Interview with author, 14 November 2018, 25 February 2019.

Newman, Mark. Phone interview with author, 20 April 2019.

Nordin, Diedre Pederson. Email to author, 31 March 2019.

Nordin, Jan. Email to author, 31 March 2019.

Nordine, Dane. "Thru the Window." *Karlstad Advocate*, 14 March 1966.

Nordine, Dane. "Dean of Basketball Will Not Be on Bench at Start of Season." *North Star News*, 15 November 1979.

Nordine, Dane. "Thru the Window." *North Star News,* 30 August 1988.

Nordine, Jon. Email to author, 21 March 2019.

Oistad, Greg. Email to author, 28 December 2018.

Olson, Keith. Email to author, 27 March 2019.

Olson, Loel. Email to author, 14 January 2019.

Olson. Lowell. Letter to editor. *North Star News,* 13 December 1979.

Olson, Tim. Emails to author: 9 July, 10 July, 12 July, 13 August 2018.

Pack, Todd. Email to author, 3 April 2019.

Pederson, Glenn.  Email to author, 15 January 2019.

Peterson, Larry.  Email to author, 24 February 2019.

Pietruszewski, Ernie.  Letter to author, 25 October 2018.

Pietruszewski, Jerry. Letter to author, 21 December 2018.

Pietruszewski, Richard.  Letter to author, 25 January 2019.

Porter, Tim.  Email to author, 24 April 2019.

Porter, Tom. Email to author, 21 April 2019.

Rasmussen, Allen.  Phone interview, 7 November, 11 November 2018.

Schindele, Jim.  Letter to author, 29 April 2019.

Schmitt, Twila.  "BHS Wins 1948 State Basketball Title." *Bemidji Pioneer*, 27 March 1988.

Schmidt, John.  Phone interview with author, 15 June 2019.

Schuler, Gary.  Letter to author. 19 February 2019.

Sele, Dan. Phone interview with author, 3 January 2019.

Sele, Lee.  Email to author, 20 March 2019.

Sjodin, Brian.  Email to author, 23 March 2019.

Sjodin, Lowell.  Emails to author, 15 October 2018, 10 -21 January, February 2, 11 February 2019.

Skogerboe, Neil.  Letter to author, 13 January 2019.

Snyder, Jerry.  Email to author, 3 April 2019.

Sparby, Eldon.  Letter to author, 19 February 2019.

Spilde, David.  Phone interview with author, 23 May 2019.

Strandquist High School Yearbook.  *Warrior 1957, 1958, 1959, 1960, 1961.*  Annual Staff.  Print.  Intercollegiate Press, Kansas City, MO.

"Strandquist Press School News." *Middle River Record*, 9 March, 16 March, 23 March, 30 March 1960.

Strandquist Warrior 1991 Final Edition. *Warrior Ninety One.*  Editor Jennifer Anderson.  Co-Editors Nicole Stromgren and Renae Blazejewski. Jostens, St. Paul, MN.

Stromlund, Rodney.  Email to author, 7 February 2019.

Szczepanski, Jerry.  Emails to author, 19 December 2018.  Interview with author, 17 May 2019.

*The Hoosiers.*  Dir. David Anspaugh.  Gene Hackman, Barbara Hershey and Dennis Hopper. De Haven Productions, 1986. DVD.

"The Warriors." *Middle River Record.*  From the Files of Jerry Szczepanski.

Ueland, Ron.  Phone interview with author, 19 March 2019, letter to author, 20 April 2019.

Urbaniak, Ken. Phone interview with author, 21 May 2019.

Vagle, Wesley. Letter to author, 11 May 2019.

Photos and articles from *North Star News (Karlstad Advocate)*and *Middle River Record* courtesy of Rollin Bergman, publisher.
Karlstad yearbook photos courtesy of Bill Champa, Champa Studio, Cold Spring, Minnesota, formerly St. Cloud, Mn. and Scott Marthaler, LeMar Photography, Wahpeton, ND, formerly Crookston, MN.
Photo of Musburger coaches at Alvarado game and photo of Warren Keller courtesy of Wayne Nelson, *Grand Forks Herald.*
Strandquist yearbook photos and photo of Jim Musburger in high school football uniform courtesy of Cooper Studios, Bemidji, Mn. and Grand Forks, N.D.
Photo of 1948 State Basketball champs courtesy of Matt Cory, *Bemidji Pioneer.*
Photo of KHS warm-up jacket courtesy of Kent Hanson.
Photo gold basketball courtesy of Mike Kuznia.
Photo of 1966 District basketball program courtesy of Ingrid Karlsson Hunnewell
Photo of Strandquist School courtesy of Darlene Gryskiewicz
Photos of Strandquist chevrons, athletic eligibility letter, and photos of raffle and supper tickets, courtesy of Jerry Szczepanski
Photo of Louis Deere courtesy of Loren Younggren, Younggren Photography, 1979 Kennedy Yearbook.

*I think the biggest thing that we took from coach is that we all became better men in life after graduation.* –Jerry Pietruszewski, '70, Karlstad